Should Trees Have Standing?

# Should Trees
# Have Standing?

## TOWARD LEGAL RIGHTS
## FOR NATURAL OBJECTS

## Christopher D. Stone

Foreword by Garrett Hardin

WILLIAM KAUFMANN, INC.

Los Altos, California

**Library of Congress Cataloging in Publication Data**

Stone, Christopher D.
   Should trees have standing?

   1. Natural resources—Law and legislation—
United States.   2. Environmental law—United
States.   I. Title.
KF5505.S86        346′.73′046        73–19535
ISBN  0–913232–09–2
ISBN  0–913232–08–4  (pbk.)

Printed in the United States of America

For my little hiking companions:

Jessica and Carey

# CONTENTS

# FOREWORD

From our ancestors we inherit three sorts of things: material objects, genes, and ideas. Of these three the first is least important, for "a fool and his money are soon parted." The other two inheritances leave more lasting traces. Genes and ideas are both stable as a rule, but the rule is normally broken at a low frequency. Genes and ideas are both mutable. The diversity created by change constitutes the field in which the forces of selection operate. On the biological plane selection is called "natural," and the result is judged "adaptation." Selection at the level of ideas goes by various names, "criticism" and "rational evaluation" among them; the results are generally referred to as "progress" (which they may indeed sometimes be).

The mutation of ideas differs strikingly from the mutation of genes in this way: change in an idea by which we have previously been unconsciously ruled becomes much more probable once the idea has been explicitly brought out into the open. Such a change in changeability does not hold for genes. The gene for the normal alternative to the disease hemophilia mutates to the hemophilic form about once in every fifty thousand opportunities, with Olympian indifference to our awareness of it.

In the mental realm, to express an idea clearly is to invite its denial. Our lives are no doubt ruled tyrannically by a wealth of ideas we have no idea of—until, without warning, we become aware of them one by one. As each ruling idea surfaces it becomes subject to a mutation process that is faster by many orders of magnitude than is the natural mutation of genes.

The foregoing assertions may sound suspiciously like the elements of a "waterproof hypothesis," since they assert the existence of unconscious forces that lose their force once they cease to be unconscious. Such a postulation would seem to be beyond proof or disproof; if so, we should refuse it admission to the realm of rational discourse. But I think the postulation is better than that. *Looking backward* we can see that we—and by "we"

I mean both ourselves and the ancestors with whom we psychologically affiliate ourselves—were formerly ruled by ideas that "we" were unconscious of at the time when the rule was effective. For example, the "divine right of kings" was calmly accepted before the phrase was invented. The invention of a legitimating phrase is often the first step to doubt and the opening of a door to the exploration of alternatives. He who explicitly asserts that kings have a divine right to rule cannot keep others from asking, "But how do you know that? And what if they don't? What would the world be like then?" In fact, the speaker cannot shield even himself against subterranean doubts once he has been so imprudent as to make a ruling assumption explicit.

Aware of tyrannical ideas we escaped in the past we cannot but wonder what unconscious ideas rule us still. How can we discover them, and so take one more step in the endless journey of escape from intellectual tyranny? There is no royal road to the discovery of the unconscious, but the economist John Maynard Keynes blazed a useful trail when he said that "a study of the history of opinion is a necessary preliminary to the emancipation of the mind." Becoming aware of the indefensible in the mental baggage of our ancestors we become sensitized to that which is dubious in our own minds.

The American naturalist Aldo Leopold opened the way to escape from one of the ideological tyrannies of our time when he made us acutely aware of the hidden implications of the terms "rights" and "property," by recounting the history recorded in the myths of Homer:

> When god-like Odysseus returned from the wars in Troy, he hanged all on one rope a dozen slave-girls of his household whom he suspected of misbehavior during his absence.
>
> This hanging involved no question of propriety. The girls were property. The disposal of property was then, as now, a matter of expediency, not of right and wrong.
>
> Concepts of right and wrong were not lacking from Odysseus' Greece: witness the fidelity of his wife through the long years before at last his black-prowed galleys clove the wine-dark seas for home. The ethical structure of that day covered wives, but had not yet been extended to human chattels. During the three thousand years which have since elapsed, ethical criteria have been extended to many fields of conduct, with corresponding shrinkages in those judged by expediency only.
>
> This extension of ethics, so far studied only by philoso-

phers, is actually a process in ecological evolution. Its sequences may be described in ecological as well as in philosophical terms. An ethic, ecologically, is a limitation on freedom of action in the struggle for existence. An ethic, philosophically, is a differentiation of social from anti-social conduct. These are two definitions of one thing. The thing has its origin in the tendency of interdependent individuals or groups to evolve modes of co-operation. The ecologist calls these symbioses. Politics and economics are advanced symbioses in which the original free-for-all competition has been replaced, in part, by co-operative mechanisms with an ethical content.

This passage,* from the essay "The Land Ethic," first published posthumously in 1949, has been often reprinted. The essay has had a great effect, first on biologists and ecologists, and latterly on the general public. Leopold went on to say:

There is as yet no ethic dealing with man's relation to land and to the animals and plants which grow upon it. Land, like Odysseus' slave-girls, is still property. The land-relation is still strictly economic, entailing privileges but not obligations.

The extension of ethics to this third element in the human environment is, if I read the evidence correctly, an evolutionary possibility and an ecological necessity. . . . Individual thinkers since the days of Ezekiel and Isaiah have asserted that the despoliation of land is not only inexpedient but wrong. Society, however, has not yet affirmed their belief. I regard the present conservation movement as the embryo of such an affirmation.

An ethic may be regarded as a mode of guidance for meeting ecological situations so new or intricate, or involving such deferred reactions, that the path of social expediency is not discernible to the average individual. Animal instincts are modes of guidance for the individual in meeting such situations. Ethics are possibly a kind of community instinct in-the-making.

The animal instincts Leopold refers to include the territorial behavior of higher animals. Animal territoriality is no doubt the progenitor of the human concept of "property," a concept which has, like all things human, undergone a wealth of varia-

---

* Taken from page 217 of Aldo Leopold, *A Sand County Almanac.* New York: Oxford University Press, 1966.

tions. Asserting that property is natural in its origin does not justify any and all of these variations. Equally natural is the concern for the welfare of other human beings that periodically brings the rights of property into question.

The most rigid defenders of the momentary legal definition of "property" apparently think "property" refers to something as substantive as atom and mass. But every good lawyer and every good economist knows that "property" is not a *thing* but merely a verbal announcement that certain traditional powers and privileges of some members of society will be vigorously defended against attack by others. Operationally, the word "property" symbolizes a threat of action; it is a verb-like entity, but (being a noun) the word biases our thoughts toward the substantives we call *things*. But the permanence enjoyed by property is not the permanence of an atom, but that of a promise (a most unsubstantial thing). Even after we become aware of the misdirection of attention enforced by the noun "property," we may still passively acquiesce to the inaccuracy of its continued use because a degree of social stability is needed to get the day-to-day work accomplished. But when it becomes painfully clear that the continued unthinking use of the word "property" is leading to consequences that are obviously unjust and socially counterproductive, then must we stop short and ask ourselves how we want to redefine the rights of property.

Law, to be stable, must be based on ethics. In evoking a new ethic to protect land and other natural amenities, Leopold implicitly called for concomitant changes in the philosophy of the law. Now, less than a generation after the publication of Leopold's classic essay, Professor Christopher D. Stone has laid the foundation for just such a philosophy in a graceful essay that itself bids fair to become a classic. The occasion of its writing was the preparation of a special issue of the *Southern California Law Review* devoted to "Law and Technology," which was published as Volume 45, Number 2 in the spring of 1972. Professor Stone later explained the background to me in detail:

> "For some time I have been thinking about the interplay between law and the development of social awareness, emphasizing to my students that societies, like human beings, progress through different stages of sensitiveness, and that in our progress through these stages the law—like art—has a role to play, dramatizing and summoning into the open the

changes that are taking place within us. While exemplifying this in class and trying to imagine what a future consciousness might look like, I began to discuss the idea of nature or natural objects being regarded as the subject of legal rights.

"The students were—to say the least—skeptical. After all, it is easy to say, 'Nature should have legal rights,' but if the notion were ever to be more than a vague sentiment, I had to find some pending case in which nature's having legal rights would make a real operational difference.

"It was in this context that I turned to the Mineral King case, then recently decided by the Ninth Circuit Court of Appeals. The U.S. Forest Service had granted a permit to Walt Disney Enterprises, Inc. to 'develop' Mineral King Valley, a wilderness area in California's Sierra Nevada Mountains, by construction of a $35 million complex of motels, restaurants, and recreational facilities. The Sierra Club, maintaining that the project would adversely affect the area's esthetic and ecological balance, brought suit for an injunction. The District Court had granted a preliminary injunction. But the Ninth Circuit reversed. The key to the Ninth Circuit's opinion was this: not that the Forest Service had been right in granting the permit, but that the Sierra Club had no "standing" to bring the question to the courts. After all, the Ninth Circuit reasoned, the Sierra Club itself

> does not allege that it is "aggrieved" or that it is "adversely affected" within the meaning of the rules of standing. Nor does the fact that no one else appears on the scene who is in fact aggrieved and is willing or desirous of taking up the cudgels create a right in appellee. The right to sue does not inure to one who does not possess it, simply because there is no one else willing and able to assert it.

"This, I saw at once, was the needed case, a ready-made vehicle to bring to the Court's attention the theory I was developing. Perhaps the injury to the Sierra Club was tenuous, but the injury to Mineral King—the park itself—wasn't. If I could get the courts thinking about the park itself as a jural person—the way corporations are "persons"—the notion of nature having rights would here make a significant operational difference—the difference between the case being heard and (the way things were then heading) thrown out of court.

"It was October 1971. The Sierra Club's appeal had already been docketed for review by the United States Supreme Court. The case, we calculated, would be up for argument in

November or December at the latest. Was it possible that we could get an article out in time to influence, perhaps, the course of the law? I sat down with Dave Boutte, then the editor of the *Southern California Law Review,* and we made some quick estimates. The next issue of the *Review* to go to press would be a special Symposium on Law and Technology, which was scheduled for publication in late March or early April. There was no hope, then, of getting an article out in time for the lawyers to work the idea into their briefs or oral arguments. Could it be published in time for the Justices to see it before they had finished deliberating and writing their opinions? The chances that the case would still be undecided in April were only slim. But there was one hope. Justice Douglas (who, if anyone on the Court, might be receptive to the notion of legal rights for natural objects) was scheduled to write the Preface to the Symposium on Law and Technology. For this reason he would be supplied with a draft of all the manuscripts in December. Thus he would at least have this idea in his hands. If the case were long enough in the deciding, and if he found the theory convincing, he might even have the article available as a source of support.

"We decided to try it. Dave made some last-minute room for my article in the Symposium and I pulled it together at a pace that, as such academic writings go, was almost breakneck. The manuscripts for the Symposium issue went to the printer in late December, and then began a long wait; the two of us hoping that—at least in this case—the wheels of justice would turn slowly. Our excitement at what happened next I leave to you to imagine."

What happened next was that the Mineral King decision was held up until 19 April 1972. On that date the United States Supreme Court (the new appointees Powell and Rehnquist not participating) upheld the Ninth Circuit. The Sierra Club itself had no sufficient "personal stake in the outcome of the controversy" to get into Court. Stone's theory (or some alternate) not having been raised, Justice Stewart, writing for the majority, did not feel called upon to pass upon its validity. But in a footnote, he dropped a broad hint: "Our decision does not, of course, bar the Sierra Club from seeking in the District Court to amend its complaint by a motion" invoking some other theory of jurisdiction.

Then came Justice Douglas's dissent. Although the theory of nature itself being the rights-holder had not been pleaded, he

decided to deal with it then and there. In his very opening paragraph—which was to resound in newspapers and editorials
across the country—he proclaimed:

> The critical question of "standing" would be simplified and
> also put neatly in focus if we fashioned a federal rule that al-
> lowed environmental issues to be litigated before federal agen-
> cies or federal courts in the name of the inanimate object
> about to be despoiled, defaced, or invaded by roads and bull-
> dozers and where injury is the subject of public outrage. Con-
> temporary public concern for protecting nature's ecological
> equilibrium should lead to the conferral of standing upon en-
> vironmental objects to sue for their own preservation. See
> Stone, Should Trees Have Standing? Toward Legal Rights for
> Natural Objects, 45 S. Cal. L. Rev. 450 (1972). This suit
> would therefore be more properly labeled as *Mineral King v.
> Morton.*

Douglas was not alone. Theretofore Justice Blackmun (a
Nixon appointee) had been in agreement with Justice Douglas
on a major issue perhaps only once, but the two were brought
together on this. Blackmun endorsed the idea in the following
terms:

> . . . Mr. Justice Douglas, in his eloquent opinion, has imag-
> inatively suggested another means [to establish standing] and
> one, in its own way, with obvious, appropriate and self-im-
> posed limitations. . . . As I read what he has written, he
> makes only one addition to the customary criteria (the exist-
> ence of a genuine dispute; the assurance of adversariness; and
> a conviction that the party whose standing is challenged will
> adequately represent the interests he asserts), that is, that the
> litigant be one who speaks knowingly for the environmental
> values he asserts.

Justice Brennan agreed.

Thus, when the dust settled, three justices had endorsed the
notion and would have "interpreted" the Sierra Club's complaint
as though it had been intended to raise Stone's thesis (conceiv-
ing Mineral King as the party in interest and the Sierra Club as
its guardian). Two judges not on the Court at the time of the
argument had abstained, and the other four (a bare majority)
had chosen not to reach the theory because it had not, technically
speaking, been raised.

In a way, the trees lost, albeit narrowly—and perhaps temporarily. Had they won, the Mineral King decision would no doubt have been called a "watershed decision." A watershed—the topographical image must be kept in mind—is ordinarily recognized only after one has passed over the ridge and is ambling down the other side. (If we haven't passed the ridge, how do we know there is one?) In the present instance, however, I submit that it is a good bet that we are near the ridge of a watershed. It is not merely the closeness of the decision (4-to-3) that leads to the suspicion; it is also the tone of the majority opinion—which is not unfriendly to the trees—as well as other evidences of a changing climate of opinion in this country. Within a month of the court's decision Senator Philip A. Hart of Michigan praised Stone's article on the floor of the Senate and received permission to have it reprinted in the Congressional Record. The rapidity with which Stone's work has been favorably commented on by jurists, journalists, and legislators gives grounds for optimism as to the early incorporation into law of Stone's thesis that natural objects should have standing in court.

Justice Blackmun, at the conclusion of his opinion, calls attention to the deep reason why change is called for when he quotes the famous lines from John Donne, "No man is an Iland . . .". (See p. 94) The poet's rhetoric does not automatically give us answers to the thousand and one practical questions with which we are daily confronted, but it does furnish a framework within which acceptable solutions may be found, namely the ecological framework. The world is a seamless web of interrelationships within which no part can, without danger, claim absolute sovereignty in rights over all other parts. Even those who agree (as not all do) with Alexander Pope that "Man is the measure of all things" must admit that man's interests are sometimes served best by taking seriously Christ's advice: "Consider the lilies of the field. . . . They toil not, neither do they spin: and yet I say unto you that even Solomon in all his glory was not arrayed like one of these." Even the narrowest view of the interests of mankind, if pursued to its farthest bound, leads us to conclude that our greatest happiness, especially if we are mindful of the survival in dignity of our posterity, demands that we give some sort of standing in court to the lilies, the trees, and all the other glories of nature.

"Poets," said John Keats, "are the unacknowledged legislators of the world." During the last two centuries the words of William

Blake, William Wordsworth, Henry David Thoreau, John Muir, John Burroughs, Rachel Carson, Aldo Leopold, and a host of others have been giving form to the statute books of our unconscious minds. But that which is unconscious is seldom precise, and in any case is not suited for action in a world of differing opinions. The statute law of the moment that is precise enough for action does not adequately take into account what many of us see as our responsibilities as trustees of the earth. Surely it is time now to make explicit the implications of the poets' insights and rebuild the written law "nearer to the heart's desire."

GARRETT HARDIN

Santa Barbara
December 1973

## PART I

*Should Trees Have Standing?*

# SHOULD TREES HAVE STANDING?— TOWARD LEGAL RIGHTS FOR NATURAL OBJECTS

CHRISTOPHER D. STONE*

## INTRODUCTION: THE UNTHINKABLE

In *Descent of Man*, Darwin observes that the history of man's moral development has been a continual extension in the objects of his "social instincts and sympathies." Originally each man had regard only for himself and those of a very narrow circle about him; later, he came to regard more and more "not only the welfare, but the happiness of all his fellowmen"; then "his sympathies became more tender and widely diffused, extending to men of all races, to the imbecile, maimed, and other useless members of society, and finally to the lower animals. . . ."[1]

The history of the law suggests a parallel development. Perhaps there never was a pure Hobbesian state of nature, in which no "rights" existed except in the vacant sense of each man's "right to self-defense." But it is not unlikely that so far as the earliest "families" (including extended kinship groups and clans) were concerned, everyone outside the family was suspect, alien, rightless.[2] And even within the family, persons we presently regard as the natural holders of at least some rights had none. Take, for example, children. We know something of the early rights-status of children from the widespread practice of infanticide—

---

* Professor of Law, University of Southern California. A.B. 1959, Harvard; LL.B. 1962, Yale. Chairman, Committee on Law and the Humanities, Association of American Law Schools. The author wishes to express his appreciation for the financial support of the National Endowment for the Humanities.

1. C. DARWIN, DESCENT OF MAN 119, 120-21 (2d ed. 1874). *See also* R. WAELDER, PROGRESS AND REVOLUTION 39 *et seq.* (1967).

2. *See* DARWIN, *supra* note 1, at 113-14:

. . . No tribe could hold together if murder, robbery, treachery, etc., were common; consequently such crimes within the limits of the same tribe "are branded with everlasting infamy"; but excite no such sentiment beyond these limits. A North-American Indian is well pleased with himself, and is honored by others, when he scalps a man of another tribe; and a Dyak cuts off the head of an unoffending person, and dries it as a trophy . . . It has been recorded that an Indian Thug conscientiously regretted that he had not robbed and strangled as many travelers as did his father before him. In a rude state of civilization the robbery of strangers is, indeed, generally considered as honorable.

*See also* Service, *Forms of Kinship* in MAN IN ADAPTATION 112 (Y. Cohen ed. 1968).

especially of the deformed and female.[3] (Senicide,[4] as among the North American Indians, was the corresponding rightlessness of the aged).[5] Maine tells us that as late as the Patria Potestas of the Romans, the father had *jus vitae necisque*—the power of life and death—over his children. A fortiori, Maine writes, he had power of "uncontrolled corporal chastisement; he can modify their personal condition at pleasure; he can give a wife to his son; he can give his daughter in marriage; he can divorce his children of either sex; he can transfer them to another family by adoption; and he can sell them." The child was less than a person: an object, a thing.[6]

The legal rights of children have long since been recognized in principle, and are still expanding in practice. Witness, just within recent time, *In re Gault*,[7] guaranteeing basic constitutional protections to juvenile defendants, and the Voting Rights Act of 1970.[8] We have been making persons of children although they were not, in law, always so. And we have done the same, albeit imperfectly some would say, with prisoners,[9] aliens, women (especially of the married variety), the insane,[10] Blacks, foetuses,[11] and Indians.

---

3. *See* DARWIN, *supra* note 1, at 113. *See also* E. WESTERMARCK, 1 THE ORIGIN AND DEVELOPMENT OF THE MORAL IDEAS 406-12 (1912).

The practice of allowing sickly children to die has not been entirely abandoned, apparently, even at our most distinguished hospitals. *See Hospital Let Retarded Baby Die, Film Shows*, L. A. Times, Oct. 17, 1971, § A, at 9, col. 1.

4. There does not appear to be a word "gericide" or "geronticide" to designate the killing of the aged. "Senicide" is as close as the Oxford English Dictionary comes, although, as it indicates, the word is rare. 9 OXFORD ENGLISH DICTIONARY 454 (1933).

5. *See* DARWIN, *supra* note 1, at 386-93. WESTERMARCK, *supra* note 3, at 387-89, observes that where the killing of the aged and infirm is practiced, it is often supported by humanitarian justification; this, however, is a far cry from saying that the killing **is** *requested* by the victim as his right.

6. H. MAINE, ANCIENT LAW 153 (Pollock ed. 1930). Maine claimed that these powers of the father extended to all regions of private law, although not to the Jus Publicum, under which a son, notwithstanding his subjection in private life, might vote alongside his father. *Id.* at 152. WESTERMARCK, *supra* note 3, at 393-94, was skeptical that the arbitrary power of the father over the children extended as late as into early Roman law.

7. 387 U.S. 1 (1967).

8. 42 U.S.C. §§ 1973 *et seq.* (1970).

9. *See* Landman v. Royster, 40 U.S.L.W. 2256 (E.D. Va., Oct. 30, 1971) (eighth amendment and due process clause of the fourteenth amendment require federal injunctive relief, including compelling the drafting of new prison rules, for Virginia prisoners against prison conduct prohibited by vague rules or no rules, without disciplinary proceedings embodying rudiments of procedural due process, and by various penalties that constitute cruel and unusual punishment). *See* Note, *Courts, Corrections and the Eighth Amendment: Encouraging Prison Reform by Releasing Inmates*, 44 S. CAL. L. REV. 1060 (1971).

Nor is it only matter in human form that has come to be recognized as the possessor of rights. The world of the lawyer is peopled with inanimate right-holders: trusts, corporations, joint ventures, municipalities, Subchapter R partnerships,[12] and nation-states, to mention just a few. Ships, still referred to by courts in the feminine gender, have long had an independent jural life, often with striking consequences.[13] We have become so accustomed to the idea of a corporation having "its" own rights, and being a "person" and "citizen" for so many statutory and constitutional purposes, that we forget how jarring the notion was to early jurists. "That invisible, intangible and artificial being, that mere legal entity" Chief Justice Marshall wrote of the corporation in *Bank of*

---

10. *But see* T. SZASZ, LAW, LIBERTY AND PSYCHIATRY (1963).

11. *See* notes 22, 52 and accompanying text *infra*. The trend toward liberalized abortion can be seen either as a legislative tendency back in the direction of rightlessness for the foetus—or toward increasing rights of women. This inconsistency is not unique in the law of course; it is simply support for Hohfeld's scheme that the "jural opposite" of someone's right is someone else's "no-right." W. HOHFELD, FUNDAMENTAL LEGAL CONCEPTIONS (1923).

Consider in this regard a New York case in which a settlor *S* established a trust on behalf of a number of named beneficiaries and "lives in being." Desiring to amend the deed of trust, the grantor took steps pursuant to statute to obtain "the written consent of all persons beneficially interested in [the] trust." At the time the grantor was pregnant and the trustee Chase Bank advised it would not recognize the proposed amendment because the child *en ventre sa mere* might be deemed a person beneficially interested in the trust. The court allowed the amendment to stand, holding that birth rather than conception is the controlling factor in ascertaining whether a person is beneficially interested in the trust which the grantor seeks to amend. *In re* Peabody, 5 N.Y.2d 541, 158 N.E.2d 841 (1959).

The California Supreme Court has recently refused to allow the deliberate killing of a foetus (in a non-abortion situation) to support a murder prosecution. The court ruled foetuses not to be denoted by the words "human being" within the statute defining murder. Keeler v. Superior Court, 2 Cal. 3d 619, 87 Cal. Rptr. 481, 470 P.2d 617 (1970). But see note 52 and accompanying text *infra*.

Some jurisdictions have statutes defining a crime of "feticide"—deliberately causing the death of an unborn child. The absence of such a specific feticide provision in the California case was one basis for the ruling in *Keeler*. *See* 2 Cal. 3d at 633 n.16, 87 Cal. Rptr. at 489 n.16, 470 P.2d at 625 n.16.

12. INT. REV. CODE of 1954, § 1361 (repealed by Pub. L. No. 89-389, effective Jan. 1, 1969).

13. For example, *see* United States v. Cargo of the Brig Malek Adhel, 43 U.S. (2 How.) 210 (1844). There, a ship had been seized and used by pirates. All this was done without the knowledge or consent of the owners of the ship. After the ship had been captured, the United States condemned and sold the "offending vessel." The owners objected. In denying release to the owners, Justice Story cited Chief Justice Marshall from an earlier case: "This is not a proceeding against the owner; it is a proceeding against the vessel for an offense committed by the vessel; which is not the less an offense . . . because it was committed without the authority and against the will of the owner." 43 U.S. at 234, quoting from United States v. Schooner Little Charles, 26 F. Cas. 979 (No. 15,612) (C.C.D. Va. 1818).

the *United States v. Deveaux*[14]—could a suit be brought in *its* name?
Ten years later, in the *Dartmouth College* case,[15] he was still refusing
to let pass unnoticed the wonder of an entity "existing only in contemplation of law."[16] Yet, long before Marshall worried over the personifying of the modern corporation, the best medieval legal scholars had
spent hundreds of years struggling with the notion of the legal nature of
those great public "corporate bodies," the Church and the State. How
could they exist in law, as entities transcending the living Pope and
King? It was clear how a king could bind *himself*—on his honor—by
a treaty. But when the king died, what was it that was burdened with
the obligations of, and claimed the rights under, the treaty *his* tangible
hand had signed? The medieval mind saw (what we have lost our
capacity to see)[17] how *unthinkable* it was, and worked out the most
elaborate conceits and fallacies to serve as anthropomorphic flesh for
the Universal Church and the Universal Empire.[18]

It is this note of the *unthinkable* that I want to dwell upon for a
moment. Throughout legal history, each successive extension of rights
to some new entity has been, theretofore, a bit unthinkable. We are
inclined to suppose the rightlessness of rightless "things" to be a decree
of Nature, not a legal convention acting in support of some status quo.
It is thus that we defer considering the choices involved in all their
moral, social, and economic dimensions. And so the United States
Supreme Court could straight-facedly tell us in *Dred Scott* that Blacks
had been denied the rights of citizenship "as a subordinate and inferior
class of beings, who had been subjugated by the dominant race. . . ."[19]

---

14.  9 U.S. (5 Cranch) 61, 86 (1809).

15.  Trustees of Darmouth College v. Woodward, 17 U.S. (4 Wheat.) 518 (1819).

16.  *Id.* at 636.

17.  Consider, for example, that the claim of the United States to the naval station
at Guantanamo Bay, at $2000-a-year rental, is based upon a treaty signed in 1903 by
José Montes for the President of Cuba and a minister representing Theodore Roosevelt; it
was subsequently ratified by two-thirds of a Senate no member of which is living today.
Lease [from Cuba] of Certain Areas for Naval or Coaling Stations, July 2, 1903, T.S. No.
426; C. BEVANS, 6 TREATIES AND OTHER INTERNATIONAL AGREEMENTS OF THE UNITED STATES
1776-1949, at 1120 (U.S. Dep't of State Pub. 8549, 1971).

18.  O. GIERKE, POLITICAL THEORIES OF THE MIDDLE AGE (Maitland transl. 1927),
especially at 22-30. The reader may be tempted to suggest that the "corporate" examples
in the text are distinguishable from environmental objects in that the former are com-
prised by and serve humans. On the contrary, I think that the more we learn about the
sociology of the firm—and the realpolitik of our society—the more we discover the ultimate reality of these institutions, and the increasingly legal fictiveness of the individual
human being. *See* note 125 and accompanying text *infra*.

19.  Dred Scott v. Sandford, 60 U.S. (19 How.) 396, 404-05 (1856). In Bailey v. Poin-
dexter's Ex'r, 56 Va. (14 Gratt.) 132, 142-43 (1858) a provision in a will that testator's

In the nineteenth century, the highest court in California explained that Chinese had not the right to testify against white men in criminal matters because they were "a race of people whom nature has marked as inferior, and who are incapable of progress or intellectual development beyond a certain point . . . between whom and ourselves nature has placed an impassable difference.[20] The popular conception of the Jew in the 13th Century contributed to a law which treated them as "men *ferae naturae*, protected by a quasi-forest law. Like the roe and the deer, they form an order apart."[21] Recall, too, that it was not so long ago that the foetus was "like the roe and the deer." In an early suit attempting to establish a wrongful death action on behalf of a negligently killed foetus (now widely accepted practice), Holmes, then on the Massachusetts Supreme Court, seems to have thought it simply inconceivable "that a man might owe a civil duty and incur a conditional prospective liability in tort to one not yet in being."[22] The first woman in Wisconsin who thought she might have a right to practice law was told that she did not, in the following terms:

> The law of nature destines and qualifies the female sex for the bearing and nurture of the children of our race and for the custody of the homes of the world . . . . [A]ll life-long callings of women, inconsistent with these radical and sacred duties of their sex, as is the profession of the law, are departures from the order of nature; and when voluntary, treason against it . . . . The

---

slaves could choose between emancipation and public sale was held void on the ground that slaves have no legal capacity to choose:

> These decisions are legal conclusions flowing naturally and necessarily from the one clear, simple, fundamental idea of chattel slavery. That fundamental idea is, that, in the eye of the law, so far certainly as civil rights and relations are concerned, the slave is not a person, but a thing. The investiture of a chattel with civil rights or legal capacity is indeed a legal solecism and absurdity. The attribution of legal personality to a chattel slave,—legal conscience, legal intellect, legal freedom, or liberty and power of free choice and action, and corresponding legal obligations growing out of such qualities, faculties and action—implies a palpable contradiction in terms.

20. People v. Hall, 4 Cal. 399, 405 (1854). The statute there under interpretation provided that "no Black or Mulatto person, or Indian shall be allowed to give evidence in favor of, or against a white man," but was silent as to Chinese. The "policy" analysis by which the court brings Chinese under "Black . . . or Indian" is a fascinating illustration of the relationship between a "policy" decision and a "just" decision, especially in light of the exchange betwen Hart, *Positivism and the Separation of Law and Morals*, 71 HARV. L. REV. 593 (1958) and Fuller, *Positivism and Fidelity to Law—A Reply to Professor Hart*, *id.* at 630.

21. Schechter, *The Rightlessness of Mediaeval English Jewry*, 45 JEWISH Q. REV. 121, 135 (1954) quoting from M. BATESON, MEDIEVAL ENGLAND 139 (1904). Schechter also quotes Henry de Bracton to the effect that "a Jew cannot have anything of his own, because whatever he acquires he acquires not for himself but for the king. . . ." *Id.* at 128.

22. Dietrich v. Inhabitants of Northampton, 138 Mass. 14, 16 (1884).

peculiar qualities of womanhood, its gentle graces, its quick sensibility, its tender susceptibility, its purity, its delicacy, its emotional impulses, its subordination of hard reason to sympathetic feeling, are surely not qualifications for forensic strife. Nature has tempered woman as little for the juridical conflicts of the court room, as for the physical conflicts of the battle field . . . .[23]

The fact is, that each time there is a movement to confer rights onto some new "entity," the proposal is bound to sound odd or frightening or laughable.[23a] This is partly because until the rightless thing receives its rights, we cannot see it as anything but a *thing* for the use of "us"—those who are holding rights at the time.[24] In this vein, what is striking about the Wisconsin case above is that the court, for all its talk about women, so clearly was never able to see women as they are

---

23. *In re* Goddell, 39 Wisc. 232, 245 (1875). The court continued with the following "clincher":

And when counsel was arguing for this lady that the word, person, in sec. 32, ch. 119 [respecting those qualified to practice law], necessarily includes females, her presence made it impossible to suggest to him as *reductio ad absurdum* of his position, that the same construction of the same word . . . would subject woman to prosecution for the paternity of a bastard, and . . . prosecution for rape.

*Id.* at 246.

The relationship between our attitudes toward woman, on the one hand, and, on the other, the more central concern of this article—land—is captured in an unguarded aside of our colleague, Curt Berger: ". . . after all, land, like woman, was meant to be possessed. . . ." LAND OWNERSHIP AND USE 139 (1968).

23a. Recently, a group of prison inmates in Suffolk County tamed a mouse that they discovered, giving him the name Morris. Discovering Morris, a jailer flushed him down the toilet. The prisoners brought a proceeding against the Warden complaining, *inter alia*, that Morris was subjected to discriminatory discharge and was otherwise unequally treated. The action was unsuccessful, on grounds that the inmates themselves were "guilty of imprisoning Morris without a charge, without a trial, and without bail," and that other mice at the prison were not treated more favorably. "As to the true victim the Court can only offer again the sympathy first proffered to his ancestors by Robert Burns. . . ." The Judge proceeded to quote from Burns' "To a Mouse." Morabito v. Cyrta, 9 CRIM. L. REP. 2472 (N.Y. Sup. Ct. Suffolk Co. Aug. 26, 1971).

The whole matter seems humorous, of course. But what we need to know more of is the function of humor in the unfolding of a culture, and the ways in which it is involved with the social growing pains to which it is testimony. Why do people make jokes about the Women's Liberation Movement? Is it not on account of—rather than in spite of—the underlying validity of the protests, and the uneasy awareness that a recognition of them is inevitable? A. Koestler rightly begins his study of the human mind, ACT OF CREATION (1964), with an analysis of humor, entitled "The Logic of Laughter." And *cf.* Freud, *Jokes and the Unconscious,* 8 STANDARD EDITION OF THE COMPLETE PSYCHOLOGICAL WORKS OF SIGMUND FREUD (J. Strachey transl. 1905). (Query too: what is the relationship between the conferring of proper *names, e.g.,* Morris, and the conferring of social and legal *rights?*)

24. Thus it was that the Founding Fathers could speak of the inalienable rights of all men, and yet maintain a society that was, by modern standards, without the most basic rights for Blacks, Indians, children and women. There was no hypocrisy; emotionally, no one *felt* that these other things were men.

(and might become). All it could see was the popular "idealized" version of *an object it needed*. Such is the way the slave South looked upon the Black.[25] There is something of a seamless web involved: there will be resistance to giving the thing "rights" until it can be seen and valued for itself; yet, it is hard to see it and value it for itself until we can bring ourselves to give it "rights"—which is almost inevitably going to sound inconceivable to a large group of people.

The reason for this little discourse on the unthinkable, the reader must know by now, if only from the title of the paper. I am quite seriously proposing that we give legal rights to forests, oceans, rivers and other so-called "natural objects" in the environment—indeed, to the natural environment as a whole.[26]

---

25. The second thought streaming from . . . the older South [is] the sincere and passionate belief that somewhere between men and cattle, God created a *tertium quid*, and called it a Negro—a clownish, simple creature, at times even lovable within its limitations, but straitly foreordained to walk within the Veil. W. E. B. DuBois, The Souls of Black Folk 89 (1924).

26. In this article I essentially limit myself to a discussion of non-animal but natural objects. I trust that the reader will be able to discern where the analysis is appropriate to advancing our understanding of what would be involved in giving "rights" to other objects not presently endowed with rights—for example, not only animals (some of which already have rights in some senses) but also humanoids, computers, and so forth. *Cf.* the National Register for Historic Places, 16 U.S.C. § 470 (1970), discussed in Ely v. Velde, 321 F. Supp. 1088 (E.D. Va. 1971).

As the reader will discover, there are large problems involved in defining the boundaries of the "natural object." For example, from time to time one will wish to speak of that portion of a river that runs through a recognized jurisdiction; at other times, one may be concerned with the entire river, or the hydrologic cycle—or the whole of nature. One's ontological choices will have a strong influence on the shape of the legal system, and the choices involved are not easy. *See* notes 49, 73 and accompanying text *infra*.

On the other hand, the problems of selecting an appropriate ontology are problems of all language—not merely of the language of legal concepts, but of ordinary language as well. Consider, for example, the concept of a "person" in legal *or* in everyday speech. Is each *person* a fixed bundle of relationships, persisting unaltered through time? Do our molecules and cells not change at every moment? Our hypostatizations always have a pragmatic quality to them. *See* D. Hume, *Of Personal Identity*, in Treatise of Human Nature bk. 1, pt. IV, § VI, in The Philosophical Works of David Hume 310-18, 324 (1854); T. Murti, The Central Philosophy of Buddhism 70-73 (1955). In Loves Body 146-47 (1966) Norman O. Brown observes:

> The existence of the "let's pretend" boundary does not prevent the continuance of the real traffic across it. Projection and introjection, the process whereby the self as distinct from the other is constituted, is not past history, an event in childhood, but a present process of continuous creation. The dualism of self and external world is built up by a constant process of reciprocal exchange between the two. The self as a stable substance enduring through time, an identity, is maintained by constantly absorbing good parts (or people) from the outside world and expelling bad parts from the inner world. "There is a continual 'unconscious' wandering of other personalities into ourselves."
> Every person, then, is many persons; a multitude made into one person; a corporate body; incorporated, a corporation. A "corporation sole"; every man

As strange as such a notion may sound, it is neither fanciful nor devoid of operational content. In fact, I do not think it would be a misdescription of recent developments in the law to say that we are already on the verge of assigning some such rights, although we have not faced up to what we are doing in those particular terms.[27] We should do so now, and begin to explore the implications such a notion would hold.

## TOWARD RIGHTS FOR THE ENVIRONMENT

Now, to say that the natural environment should have rights is not to say anything as silly as that no one should be allowed to cut down a tree. We say human beings have rights, but—at least as of the time of this writing—they can be executed.[28] Corporations have rights, but they cannot plead the fifth amendment;[29] *In re Gault* gave 15-year-olds certain rights in juvenile proceedings, but it did not give them the right to vote. Thus, to say that the environment should have rights is not to say that it should have every right we can imagine, or even the same body of rights as human beings have. Nor is it to say that everything in the

---

a parson-person. The unity of the person is as real, or unreal, as the unity of the corporation.
*See generally*, W. BISHIN & C. STONE, LAW, LANGUAGE AND ETHICS Ch. 5 (1972).

In different legal systems at different times, there have been many shifts in the entity deemed "responsible" for harmful acts: an entire clan was held responsible for a crime before the notion of individual responsibility emerged; in some societies the offending hand, rather than an entire body, may be "responsible." Even today, we treat father and son as separate jural entities for some purposes, but as a single jural entity for others. I do not see why, in principle, the task of working out a legal ontology of natural objects (and "qualities," *e.g.*, climatic warmth) should be any more unmanageable. Perhaps someday all mankind shall be, for some purposes, one jurally recognized "natural object."

27. The statement in text is not quite true; *cf.* Murphy, *Has Nature Any Right to Life?*, 22 HAST. L.J. 467 (1971). An Irish court, passing upon the validity of a testamentary trust to the benefit of someone's dogs, observed in dictum that " 'lives' means lives of human beings, not of animals or trees in California." Kelly v. Dillon, 1932 Ir. R. 255, 261. (The intended gift over on the death of the last surviving dog was held void for remoteness, the court refusing "to enter into the question of a dog's expectation of life," although prepared to observe that "in point of fact neighbor's [sic] dogs and cats are unpleasantly long-lived. . . ." *Id.* at 260-61).

28. Four cases dealing with the Constitutionality of the death penalty under the eighth and fourteenth amendments are pending before the United States Supreme Court. Branch v. Texas, 447 S.W.2d 932 (Tex. 1969), *cert. granted*, 91 S. Ct. 2287 (1970); Aikens v. California, 70 Cal. 2d 369, 74 Cal. Rptr. 882, 450 P.2d 258 (1969), *cert. granted*, 91 S. Ct. 2280 (1970); Furman v. Georgia, 225 Ga. 253, 167 S.E.2d 628 (1969), *cert. granted*, 91 S. Ct. 2282 (1970); Jackson v. Georgia, 225 Ga. 790, 171 S.E.2d 501 (1969), *cert. granted*, 91 S. Ct. 2287 (1970).

29. *See* George Campbell Painting Corp. v. Reid, 392 U.S. 286 (1968); Oklahoma Press Pub. Co. v. Walling, 327 U.S. 186 (1946); Baltimore & O.R.R. v. ICC, 221 U.S. 612 (1911); Wilson v. United States, 221 U.S. 361 (1911); Hale v. Henkel, 201 U.S. 43 (1906).

environment should have the same rights as every other thing in the environment.

What the granting of rights does involve has two sides to it. The first involves what might be called the legal-operational aspects; the second, the psychic and socio-psychic aspects. I shall deal with these aspects in turn.

## THE LEGAL-OPERATIONAL ASPECTS

### What it Means to be a Holder of Legal Rights

There is, so far as I know, no generally accepted standard for how one ought to use the term "legal rights." Let me indicate how I shall be using it in this piece.

First and most obviously, if the term is to have any content at all, an entity cannot be said to hold a legal right unless and until *some public authoritative body* is prepared to give *some amount of review* to actions that are colorably inconsistent with that "right." For example, if a student can be expelled from a university and cannot get any public official, even a judge or administrative agent at the lowest level, either (i) to require the university to justify its actions (if only to the extent of filling out an affidavit alleging that the expulsion "was not wholly arbitrary and capricious") or (ii) to compel the university to accord the student some procedural safeguards (a hearing, right to counsel, right to have notice of charges), then the minimum requirements for saying that the student has a legal right to his education do not exist.[30]

But for a thing to be *a holder of legal rights*, something more is needed than that some authoritative body will review the actions and processes of those who threaten it. As I shall use the term, "holder of legal rights," each of three additional criteria must be satisfied. All three, one will observe, go towards making a thing *count* jurally—to have a legally recognized worth and dignity in its own right, and not merely to serve as a means to benefit "us" (whoever the contemporary group of rights-holders may be). They are, first, that the thing can institute legal actions *at its behest*; second, that in determining the granting of legal relief, the court must take *injury to it* into account; and, third, that relief must run to the *benefit of it*.

To illustrate, even as between two societies that condone slavery

---

30. *See* Dixon v. Alabama State Bd. of Educ., 294 F.2d 150 (5th Cir.), *cert. denied*, 368 U.S. 930 (1961).

there is a fundamental difference between $S_1$, in which a master can (if he chooses), go to court and collect reduced chattel value damages from someone who has beaten his slave, and $S_2$, in which the slave can institute the proceedings *himself*, for *his* own recovery, damages being measured by, say, *his* pain and suffering. Notice that neither society is so structured as to leave wholly unprotected the slave's interests in not being beaten. But in $S_2$ as opposed to $S_1$ there are three operationally significant advantages that the slave has, and these make the slave in $S_2$, albeit a slave, a holder of rights. Or, again, compare two societies, $S_1$, in which pre-natal injury to a live-born child gives a right of action against the tortfeasor at the mother's instance, for the mother's benefit, on the basis of the mother's mental anguish, and $S_2$, which gives the child a suit in its own name (through a guardian *ad litem*) for its own recovery, for damages to it.

When I say, then, that at common law "natural objects" are not holders of legal rights, I am not simply remarking what we would all accept as obvious. I mean to emphasize three specific legal-operational advantages that the environment lacks, leaving it in the position of the slave and the foetus in $S_1$, rather than the slave and foetus of $S_2$.

### The Rightlessness of Natural Objects at Common Law

Consider, for example, the common law's posture toward the pollution of a stream. True, courts have always been able, in some circumstances, to issue orders that will stop the pollution—just as the legal system in $S_1$ is so structured as incidentally to discourage beating slaves and being reckless around pregnant women. But the stream itself is fundamentally rightless, with implications that deserve careful reconsideration.

The first sense in which the stream is not a rights-holder has to do with standing. The stream itself has none. So far as the common law is concerned, there is in general no way to challenge the polluter's actions save at the behest of a lower riparian—another human being—able to show an invasion of *his* rights. This conception of the riparian as the holder of the right to bring suit has more than theoretical interest. The lower riparians may simply not care about the pollution. They themselves may be polluting, and not wish to stir up legal waters. They may be economically dependent on their polluting neighbor.[31] And, of

---

31. For example, *see* People *ex rel.* Ricks Water Co. v. Elk River Mill & Lumber Co., 107 Cal. 221, 40 Pac. 531 (1895) (refusing to enjoin pollution by a upper riparian at the instance of the Attorney General on the grounds that the lower riparian owners, most of whom were dependent on the lumbering business of the polluting mill, did not complain).

course, when they discount the value of winning by the costs of bringing suit and the chances of success, the action may not seem worth undertaking. Consider, for example, that while the polluter might be injuring 100 downstream riparians $10,000 a year *in the aggregate*, each riparian separately might be suffering injury only to the extent of $100—possibly not enough for any one of them to want to press suit by himself, or even to go to the trouble and cost of securing co-plaintiffs to make it worth everyone's while. This hesitance will be especially likely when the potential plaintiffs consider the burdens the law puts in their way:[32] proving, *e.g.*, specific damages, the "unreasonableness" of defendant's use of the water, the fact that practicable means of abatement exist, and overcoming difficulties raised by issues such as joint causality, right to pollute by prescription, and so forth. Even in states which, like California, sought to overcome these difficulties by empowering the attorney-general to sue for abatement of pollution in limited instances, the power has been sparingly invoked and, when invoked, narrowly construed by the courts.[33]

The second sense in which the common law denies "rights" to natural objects has to do with the way in which the merits are decided in those cases in which someone is competent and willing to establish standing. At its more primitive levels, the system protected the "rights" of the property owning human with minimal weighing of any values: *"Cujus est solum, ejus est usque ad coelum et ad infernos."*[34] Today we have come more and more to make balances—but only such as will adjust the economic best interests of identifiable humans. For example, continuing with the case of streams, there are commentators who speak of a "general rule" that "a riparian owner is legally entitled to have the stream flow by his land with its quality unimpaired" and observe that "an upper owner has, prima facie, no right to pollute the water."[35]

---

32. The law in a suit for injunctive relief is commonly easier on the plaintiff than in a suit for damages. *See* J. GOULD, LAW OF WATERS § 206 (1883).

33. However, in 1970 California amended its Water Quality Act to make it easier for the Attorney General to obtain relief, *e.g.*, one must no longer allege irreparable injury in a suit for an injunction. CAL. WATER CODE § 13350(b) (West 1971).

34. To whomsoever the soil belongs, he owns also to the sky and to the depths. *See* W. BLACKSTONE, 2 COMMENTARIES *18.

At early common law, the owner of land could use all that was found under his land "at his free will and pleasure" without regard to any "inconvenience to his neighbour." Acton v. Blundell, 12 Meeson & Welsburg 324, 354, 152 Eng. Rep. 1223, 1235 (1843). "He [the landowner] may waste or despoil the land as he pleases. . . ." R. MEGARRY & H. WADE, THE LAW OF REAL PROPERTY 70 (3d ed. 1966). *See* R. POWELL, 5 THE LAW OF REAL PROPERTY ¶725 (1971).

35. *See* Note, *Statutory Treatment of Industrial Stream Pollution*, 24 GEO. WASH.

Such a doctrine, if strictly invoked, would protect the stream absolutely whenever a suit was brought; but obviously, to look around us, the law does not work that way. Almost everywhere there are doctrinal qualifications on riparian "rights" to an unpolluted stream.[36] Although these rules vary from jurisdiction to jurisdiction, and upon whether one is suing for an equitable injunction or for damages, what they all have in common is some sort of balancing. Whether under language of "reasonable use," "reasonable methods of use," "balance of convenience" or "the public interest doctrine,"[37] what the courts are balancing, with varying degrees of directness, are the economic hardships on the upper riparian (or dependent community) of abating the pollution vis-à-vis the economic hardships of continued pollution on the lower riparians. What does not weigh in the balance is the damage to the stream, its fish and turtles and "lower" life. So long as the natural environment itself is rightless, these are not matters for judicial cognizance. Thus, we find the highest court of Pennsylvania refusing to stop a coal company from discharging polluted mine water into a tributary of the Lackawana River because a plaintiff's "grievance is for a mere personal inconvenience; and . . . mere private personal inconveniences . . . must yield to the necessities of a great public industry, which although in the hands of a private corporation, subserves a great public interest."[38] The stream itself is lost sight of in "a quantitative compromise between *two* conflicting interests."[39]

The third way in which the common law makes natural objects rightless has to do with who is regarded as the beneficiary of a favorable judgment. Here, too, it makes a considerable difference that it is not

---

L. REV. 302, 306 (1955); H. FARNHAM, 2 LAW OF WATERS AND WATER RIGHTS § 461 (1904); GOULD, *supra* note 32, at § 204.

36. For example, courts have upheld a right to pollute by prescription, Mississippi Mills Co. v. Smith, 69 Miss. 299, 11 So. 26 (1882), and by easement, Luama v. Bunker Hill & Sullivan Mining & Concentrating Co., 41 F.2d 358 (9th Cir. 1930).

37. *See* Red River Roller Mills v. Wright, 30 Minn. 249, 15 N.W. 167 (1883) (enjoyment of stream by riparian may be modified or abrogated by reasonable use of stream by others); Townsend v. Bell, 167 N.Y. 462, 60 N.E. 757 (1901) (riparian owner not entitled to maintain action for pollution of stream by factory where he could not show use of water was unreasonable); Smith v. Staso Milling Co., 18 F.2d 736 (2d Cir. 1927) (in suit for injunction, right on which injured lower riparian stands is a quantitative compromise between two conflicting interests); Clifton Iron Co. v. Dye, 87 Ala. 468, 6 So. 192 (1889) (in determining whether to grant injunction to lower riparian, court must weigh interest of public as against injury to one or the other party). *See also* Montgomery Limestone Co. v. Bearder, 256 Ala. 269, 54 So. 2d 571 (1951).

38. Pennsylvania Coal Co. v. Sanderson, 113 Pa. 126, 149, 6 A. 453, 459 (1886).

39. Hand, J. in Smith v. Staso Milling Co., 18 F.2d 736, 738 (2d Cir. 1927) (emphasis added). *See also* Harrisonville v. Dickey Clay Co., 289 U.S. 334 (1933) (Brandeis, J.).

the natural object that counts in its own right. To illustrate this point, let me begin by observing that it makes perfectly good sense to speak of, and ascertain, the legal damage to a natural object, if only in the sense of "making it whole" with respect to the most obvious factors.[40] The costs of making a forest whole, for example, would include the costs of reseeding, repairing watersheds, restocking wildlife—the sorts of costs the Forest Service undergoes after a fire. Making a polluted stream whole would include the costs of restocking with fish, water-fowl, and other animal and vegetable life, dredging, washing out impurities, establishing natural and/or artificial aerating agents, and so forth. Now, what is important to note is that, under our present system, even if a plaintiff riparian wins a water pollution suit for damages, no money goes to the benefit of the stream itself to repair *its* damages.[41] This omission has the further effect that, at most, the law confronts a polluter with what it takes to make the plaintiff riparians whole; this may be far less than the damages to the stream,[42] but not so much as to force the polluter to desist. For example, it is easy to imagine a polluter whose activities damage a stream to the extent of $10,000 annually, although the aggregate damage to all the riparian plaintiffs who come into the suit is only $3000. If $3000 is less than the cost to the polluter of shutting down, or making the requisite technological changes, he might prefer to pay off the damages (*i.e.*, the legally cognizable damages) and continue to pollute the stream. Similarly, even if the jurisdiction issues an injunction at the plaintiffs' behest (rather than to order payment of damages), there is nothing to stop the plaintiffs from "selling out" the stream, *i.e.*, agreeing to dissolve or not enforce the injunction at some price (in the example above, somewhere between plaintiffs' damages—$3000—and defendant's next best economic alternative). Indeed, I take it this is exactly what Learned Hand had in mind in an opinion in which, after issuing an anti-pollution injunction, he suggests that the defendant

---

40. Measuring plantiff's damages by "making him whole" has several limitations; these and the matter of measuring damages in this area generally are discussed more fully at notes 83-93 and accompanying text *infra*.

41. Here, again, an analogy to corporation law might be profitable. Suppose that in the instance of negligent corporate management by the directors, there were no institution of the stockholder derivative suit to force the directors to make *the corporation* whole, and the only actions provided for were direct actions by stockholders to collect for damages *to themselves qua* stockholders. Theoretically and practically, the damages might come out differently in the two cases, and not merely because the creditors' losses are not aggregated in the stockholders' direct actions.

42. And even far less than the damages to all human economic interests derivately through the stream; *see* text accompanying notes 83-84, 120 *infra*.

"make its peace with the plaintiff as best it can."[43] What is meant is a peace between *them*, and not amongst them and the river.

I ought to make clear at this point that the common law as it affects streams and rivers, which I have been using as an example so far, is not exactly the same as the law affecting other environmental objects. Indeed, one would be hard pressed to say that there was a "typical" environmental object, so far as its treatment at the hands of the law is concerned. There are some differences in the law applicable to all the various resources that are held in common: rivers, lakes, oceans, dunes, air, streams (surface and subterranean), beaches, and so forth.[44] And there is an even greater difference as between these traditional communal resources on the one hand, and natural objects on traditionally private land, *e.g.*, the pond on the farmer's field, or the stand of trees on the suburbanite's lawn.

On the other hand, although there be these differences which would make it fatuous to generalize about a law of the natural environment, most of these differences simply underscore the points made in the instance of rivers and streams. None of the natural objects, whether held in common or situated on private land, has any of the three criteria of a rights-holder. They have no standing in their own right; their unique damages do not count in determining outcome; and they are not the beneficiaries of awards. In such fashion, these objects have traditionally been regarded by the common law, and even by all but the most recent legislation, as objects for man to conquer and master and use—in such a way as the law once looked upon "man's" relationships to African Negroes. Even where special measures have been taken to conserve them, as by seasons on game and limits on timber cutting, the dominant motive has been to conserve them *for us*—for the greatest good of the greatest number of human beings. Conservationists, so far as I am aware, are generally reluctant to maintain otherwise.[45] As the name implies, they want to conserve and guarantee *our* consumption and *our* enjoyment of these other living things. In their own right, natural objects have counted for little, in law as in popular movements.

---

43.   Smith v. Staso, 18 F.2d 736, 738 (2d Cir. 1927).

44.   Some of these public properties are subject to the "public trust doctrine," which, while ill-defined, might be developed in such fashion as to achieve fairly broad-ranging environmental protection. *See* Gould v. Greylock Reservation Comm'n, 350 Mass. 410, 215 N.E.2d 114 (1966), discussed in Sax, *The Public Trust Doctrine in Natural Resource Law: Effective Judicial Intervention*, 68 MICH. L. REV. 471, 492-509 (1970).

45.   By contrast, for example, with humane societies.

As I mentioned at the outset, however, the rightlessness of the natural environment can and should change; it already shows some signs of doing so.

## Toward Having Standing in its Own Right

It is not inevitable, nor is it wise, that natural objects should have no rights to seek redress in their own behalf. It is no answer to say that streams and forests cannot have standing because streams and forests cannot speak. Corporations cannot speak either; nor can states, estates, infants, incompetents, muncipalities or universities. Lawyers speak for them, as they customarily do for the ordinary citizen with legal problems. One ought, I think, to handle the legal problems of natural objects as one does the problems of legal incompetents—human beings who have become vegetable. If a human being shows signs of becoming senile and has affairs that he is de jure incompetent to manage, those concerned with his well being make such a showing to the court, and someone is designated by the court with the authority to manage the incompetent's affairs. The guardian[46] (or "conservator"[47] or "committee"[48]—the terminology varies) then represents the incompetent in his legal affairs. Courts make similar appointments when a corporation has become "incompetent"—they appoint a trustee in bankruptcy or reorganization to oversee its affairs and speak for it in court when that becomes necessary.

On a parity of reasoning, we should have a system in which, when a friend of a natural object perceives it to be endangered, he can apply to a court for the creation of a guardianship.[49] Perhaps we already

---

46. *See, e.g.*, CAL. PROB. CODE §§ 1460-62 (West Supp. 1971).

47. CAL. PROB. CODE § 1751 (West Supp. 1971) provides for the appointment of a "conservator."

48. In New York the Supreme Court and county courts outside New York City have jurisdiction to appoint a committee of the person and/or a committee of the property for a person "incompetent to manage himself or his affairs." N.Y. MENTAL HYGIENE LAW § 100 (McKinney 1971).

49. This is a situation in which the ontological problems discussed in note 26 *supra* become acute. One can conceive a situation in which a guardian would be appointed by a county court with respect to a stream, bring a suit against alleged polluters, and lose. Suppose now that a federal court were to appoint a guardian with respect to the larger river system of which the stream were a part, and that the federally appointed guardian subsequently were to bring suit against the same defendants in state court, now on behalf of the river, rather than the stream. (Is it possible to bring a still subsequent suit, if the one above fails, on behalf of the entire hydrologic cycle, by a guardian appointed by an international court?)

While such problems are difficult, they are not impossible to solve. For one thing, pre-trial hearings and rights of intervention can go far toward their amelioration. Further, courts have been dealing with the matter of potentially inconsistent judgments

have the machinery to do so. California law, for example, defines an incompetent as "any person, whether insane or not, who by reason of old age, disease, weakness of mind, or other cause, is unable, unassisted, properly to manage and take care of himself or his property, and by reason thereof is likely to be deceived or imposed upon by artful or designing persons."[50] Of course, to urge a court that an endangered river is "a person" under this provision will call for lawyers as bold and imaginative as those who convinced the Supreme Court that a railroad corporation was a "person" under the fourteenth amendment, a constitutional provision theretofore generally thought of as designed to secure the rights of freedmen.[51] (As this article was going to press, Professor Byrn of Fordham petitioned the New York Supreme Court to appoint him legal guardian for an unrelated foetus scheduled for abortion so as to enable him to bring a class action on behalf of all foetuses similarly situated in New York City's 18 municipal hospitals. Judge Holtzman granted the petition of guardianship.[52]) If such an argument based on present statutes should fail, special environmental legislation could be enacted along traditional guardianship lines. Such provisions could provide for guardianship both in the instance of public natural objects and also, perhaps with slightly different standards, in the instance of natural objects on "private" land.[53]

---

for years, as when one state appears on the verge of handing down a divorce decree inconsistent with the judgment of another state's courts. Kempson v. Kempson, 58 N.J. Eg. 94, 43 A. 97 (Ch. Ct. 1899). Courts could, and of course would, retain some natural objects in the res nullius classification to help stave off the problem. Then, too, where (as is always the case) several "objects" are interrelated, several guardians could all be involved, with procedures for removal to the appropriate court—probably that of the guadian of the most encompassing "ward" to be acutely threatened. And in some cases subsequent suit by the guardian of more encompassing ward, not guilty of laches, might be appropriate. The problems are at least no more complex than the corresponding problems that the law has dealt with for years in the class action area.

50. CAL. PROB. CODE § 1460 (West Supp. 1971). The N.Y. MENTAL HYGIENE LAW (McKinney 1971) provides for jurisdiction "over the custody of a person and his property if he is incompetent to manage himself or his affairs by reason of age, drunkenness, mental illness or other cause. . . ."

51. Santa Clara County v. Southern Pac. R.R., 118 U.S. 394 (1886). Justice Black would have denied corporations the rights of "persons" under the fourteenth amendment. See Connecticut Gen. Life Ins. Co. v. Johnson, 303 U.S. 77, 87 (1938) (Black, J. dissenting): "Corporations have neither race nor color."

52. In re Byrn, L. A. Times, Dec. 5, 1971, § 1, at 16, col. 1. A preliminary injunction was subsequently granted, and defendant's cross-motion to vacate the guardianship was denied. Civ. 13113/71 (Sup. Ct. Queens Co., Jan. 4, 1972) (Smith, J.). Appeals are pending. Granting a guardianship in these circumstances would seem to be a more radical advance in the law than granting a guardianship over communal natural objects like lakes. In the former case there is a traditionally recognized guardian for the object—the mother—and her decision has been in favor of aborting the foetus.

53. The laws regarding the various communal resources had to develop along their own lines, not only because so many different persons' "rights" to consumption and

The potential "friends" that such a statutory scheme would require will hardly be lacking. The Sierra Club, Environmental Defense Fund, Friends of the Earth, Natural Resources Defense Counsel, and the Izaak Walton League are just some of the many groups which have manifested unflagging dedication to the environment and which are becoming increasingly capable of marshalling the requisite technical experts and lawyers. If, for example, the Environmental Defense Fund should have reason to believe that some company's strip mining operations might be irreparably destroying the ecological balance of large tracts of land, it could, under this procedure, apply to the court in which the lands were situated to be appointed guardian.[54] As guardian, it might be given rights of inspection (or visitation) to determine and bring to the court's attention a fuller finding on the land's condition. If there were indications that under the substantive law some redress might be available on the land's behalf, then the guardian would be entitled to raise the land's rights in the land's name, *i.e.*, without having to make the roundabout and often unavailing demonstration, discussed below, that the "rights" of the club's members were being invaded. Guardians would also be looked to for a host of other protective tasks, *e.g.*, monitoring effluents (and/or monitoring the monitors), and representing their "wards" at legislative and administrative hearings on such matters as the setting of state water quality standards. Procedures exist, and can be strengthened, to move a court for the removal and substi-

---

usage were continually and contemporaneously involved, but also because no one had to bear the costs of his consumption of public resources in the way in which the owner of resources on private land has to bear the costs of what he does. For example, if the landowner strips his land of trees, and puts nothing in their stead, he confronts the costs of what he has done in the form of reduced value of his land; but the river polluter's actions are costless, so far as he is concerned—except insofar as the legal system can somehow force him to internalize them. The result has been that the private landowner's power over natural objects on his land is far less restrained by law (as opposed to economics) than his power over the public resources that he can get his hands on. If this state of affairs is to be changed, the standard for interceding in the interests of natural objects on traditionally recognized "private" land might well parallel the rules that guide courts in the matter of people's children whose upbringing (or lack thereof) poses social threat. The courts can, for example, make a child "a dependent of the court" where the child's "home is an unfit place for him by reason of neglect, cruelty, or depravity of either of his parents. . . ." CAL. WELF. & INST. CODE § 600(b) (West 1966). *See also id* at § 601: any child "who from any cause is in danger of leading an idle, dissolute, lewd, or immoral life [may be adjudged] a ward of the court."

54. *See* note 53 *supra*. The present way of handling such problems on "private" property is to try to enact legislation of general application under the police power, *see* Pennsylvania Coal Co. v. Mahon, 260 U.S. 393 (1922), rather than to institute civil litigation which, though a piecemeal process, can be tailored to individual situations.

tution of guardians, for conflicts of interest or for other reasons,[55] as well as for the termination of the guardianship.[56]

In point of fact, there is a movement in the law toward giving the environment the benefits of standing, although not in a manner as satisfactory as the guardianship approach. What I am referring to is the marked liberalization of traditional standing requirements in recent cases in which environmental action groups have challenged federal government action. *Scenic Hudson Preservation Conference v. FPC*[57] is a good example of this development. There, the Federal Power Commission had granted New York's Consolidated Edison a license to construct a hydroelectric project on the Hudson River at Storm King Mountain. The grant of license had been opposed by conservation interests on the grounds that the transmission lines would be unsightly, fish would be destroyed, and nature trails would be inundated. Two of these conservation groups, united under the name Scenic Hudson Preservation Conference, petitioned the Second Circuit to set aside the grant. Despite the claim that Scenic Hudson had no standing because it had not made the traditional claim "of any personal economic injury resulting from the Commission's actions,"[58] the petitions were heard, and the case sent back to the Commission. On the standing point, the court noted that Section 313(b) of the Federal Power Act gave a right of instituting review to any party "aggrieved by an order issued by the Commission";[59] it thereupon read "aggrieved by" as not limited to those alleging the traditional personal economic injury, but as broad enough to include "those who by their activities and conduct have exhibited a special interest" in "the aesthetic, conservational, and recreational aspects of power development. . . ."[60] A similar reasoning has

---

55. CAL. PROB. CODE § 1580 (West Supp. 1971) lists specific causes for which a guardian may, after notice and a hearing, be removed.

Despite these protections, the problem of overseeing the guardian is particularly acute where, as here, there are no immediately identifiable human beneficiaries whose self-interests will encourage them to keep a close watch on the guardian. To ameliorate this problem, a page might well be borrowed from the law of ordinary charitable trusts, which are commonly placed under the supervision of the Attorney General. *See* CAL. CORP. CODE §§ 9505, 10207 (West 1955).

56. *See* CAL. PROB. CODE §§ 1472, 1590 (West 1956 and Supp. 1971).

57. 354 F.2d 608 (2d Cir. 1965), *cert. denied*, Consolidated Edison Co. v. Scenic Hudson Preservation Conf., 384 U.S. 941 (1966).

58. 354 F.2d 608, 615 (2d Cir. 1965).

59. Act of Aug. 26, 1935, ch. 687, Title II, § 213, 49 Stat. 860 (*codified in* 16 U.S.C. § 8251(b) (1970).

60. 354 F.2d 608, 616 (2d Cir. 1965). The court might have felt that because the New York-New Jersey Trial Conference, one of the two conservation groups that

swayed other circuits to allow proposed actions by the Federal Power Commission, the Department of Interior, and the Department of Health, Education and Welfare to be challenged by environmental action groups on the basis of, *e.g.*, recreational and esthetic interests of members, in lieu of direct economic injury.[61] Only the Ninth Circuit has balked, and one of these cases, involving the Sierra Club's attempt to challenge a Walt Disney development in the Sequoia National Forest, is at the time of this writing awaiting decision by the United States Supreme Court.[62]

organized Scenic Hudson, had some 17 miles of trailways in the area of Storm King Mountain, it therefore had sufficient economic interest to establish standing; Judge Hays' opinion does not seem to so rely, however.

61. Road Review League v. Boyd, 270 F. Supp. 650 (S.D.N.Y. 1967). Plaintiffs who included the Town of Bedford and the Road Review League, a non-profit association concerned with community problems, brought an action to review and set aside a determination of the Federal Highway Administrator concerning the alignment of an interstate highway. Plaintiffs claimed that the proposed road would have an adverse effect upon local wildlife sanctuaries, pollute a local lake, and be inconsistent with local needs and planning. Plaintiffs relied upon the section of the Administrative Procedure Act, 5 U.S.C. § 702 (1970), which entitles persons "aggrieved by agency action within the meaning of a relevant statute" to obtain judicial review. The court held that plaintiffs had standing to obtain judicial review of proposed alignment of the road:

> I see no reason why the word "aggrieved" should have different meaning in the Administrative Procedure Act from the meaning given it under the Federal Power Act. . . . The "relevant statute," i.e., the Federal Highways Act, contains language which seems even stronger than that of the Federal Power Act, as far as local and conservation interests are concerned.

*Id.* at 661.

In Citizens Comm. for the Hudson Valley v. Volpe, 425 F.2d 97 (2d Cir. 1970), plaintiffs were held to have standing to challenge the construction of a dike and causeway adjacent to the Hudson Valley. The Sierra Club and the Village of Tarrytown based their challenge upon the provisions of the Rivers and Harbors Act of 1899. While the Rivers and Harbors Act does not provide for judicial review as does the Federal Power Act, the court stated that the plaintiffs were "aggrieved" under the Department of Transportation Act, the Hudson River Basin Compact Act, and a regulation under which the Corps of Engineers issued a permit, all of which contain broad provisions mentioning recreational and environmental resources and the need to preserve the same. Citing the *Road Review League* decision, the court held that as "aggrieved" parties under the Administrative Procedure Act, plaintiffs similarly had standing. Other decisions in which the court's grant of standing was based upon the Administrative Procedure Act include: West Virginia Highlands Conservancy v. Island Creek Coal Co., 441 F.2d 231 (4th Cir. 1971); Environmental Defense Fund, Inc. v. Hardin, 428 F.2d 1093 (D.C. Cir. 1970); Allen v. Hickel, 424 F.2d 944 (D.C. Cir. 1970); Brooks v. Volpe, 329 F. Supp. 118 (W.D. Wash. 1971); Delaware v. Pennsylvania N.Y. Cent. Transp. Co., 323 F. Supp. 487 (D. Del. 1971); Izaak Walton League of America v. St. Clair, 313 F. Supp. 1312 (D. Minn. 1970); Pennsylvania Environmental Council, Inc. v. Bartlett, 315 F. Supp. 238 (M.D. Pa. 1970).

62. Sierra Club v. Hickel, 433 F.2d 24 (9th Cir. 1970), *cert. granted sub nom.* Sierra Club v. Morton, 401 U.S. 907 (1971) (No. 70-34). The Sierra Club, a non-profit California corporation concerned with environmental protection, claimed that its interest in the conservation and sound management of natural parks would be adversely affected by an Interior permit allowing Walt Disney to construct the Mineral King Resort in Sequoia

Even if the Supreme Court should reverse the Ninth Circuit in the Walt Disney-Sequoia National Forest matter, thereby encouraging the circuits to continue their trend toward liberalized standing in this area, there are significant reasons to press for the guardianship approach notwithstanding. For one thing, the cases of this sort have extended standing on the basis of interpretations of specific federal statutes—the Federal Power Commission Act,[63] the Administrative Procedure Act,[64] the Federal Insecticide, Fungicide and Rodenticide Act,[65] and others. Such a basis supports environmental suits only where acts of federal agencies are involved; and even there, perhaps, only when there is some special statutory language, such as "aggrieved by" in the Federal Power Act, on which the action groups can rely. Witness, for example, *Bass Angler Sportsman Society v. United States Steel Corp.*[66] There, plaintiffs sued 175 corporate defendants located throughout Alabama, relying on 33 U.S.C. § 407 (1970), which provides:

> It shall not be lawful to throw, discharge, or deposit . . . any refuse matter . . . into any navigable water of the United States, or into any tributary of any navigable water from which the same shall float or be washed into such navigable water. . . .[67]

Another section of the Act provides that one-half the fines shall be paid to the person or persons giving information which shall lead to a conviction.[68] Relying on this latter provision, the plaintiff designated his action a *qui tam* action[69] and sought to enforce the Act by injunction

---

National Forest. The court held that because of the Sierra Club's failure to assert a direct legal interest, that organization lacked standing to sue. The court stated that the Sierra Club had claimed an interest only in the sense that the proposed course of action was displeasing to its members. The court purported to distinguish *Scenic Hudson* on the grounds that the plaintiff's claim of standing there was aided by the "aggrieved party" language of the Federal Power Act.

63.  16 U.S.C. §§ 791(a) *et seq.* (1970). *See* note 59 and accompanying text *supra.*

64.  5 U.S.C. §§ 551 *et seq.* (1970). Decisions relying upon 5 U.S.C. § 702 are listed in note 56 *supra.*

65.  7 U.S.C. §§ 135 *et seq.* (1970). Section 135b(d) affords a right of judicial review to anyone "adversely affected" by an order under the Act. *See* Environmental Defense Fund, Inc. v. Hardin, 428 F.2d 1093, 1096 (D.C. Cir. 1970).

66.  324 F. Supp. 412 (N.D., M.D. & S.D. Ala. 1970), *aff'd mem., sub nom.* Bass Anglers Sportsman Soc'y of America, Inc. v. Koppers Co., 447 F.2d 1304 (5th Cir. 1971).

67.  Section 13 of Rivers and Harbors Appropriation Act of 1899.

68.  33 U.S.C. § 411 (1970) reads:

Every person and every corporation that shall violate, or that shall knowingly aid, abet, authorize, or instigate a violation of the provisions of sections 407, 408, and 409 of the title shall . . . be punished by a fine . . . or by imprisonment . . . in the discretion of the court, one-half of said fine to be paid to the person or persons giving information which shall lead to conviction.

69.  This is from the latin, "who brings the action as well for the King as for himself," referring to an action brought by a citizen for the state as well as for himself.

and fine. The District Court ruled that, in the absence of express language to the contrary, no one outside the Department of Justice had standing to sue under a criminal act and refused to reach the question of whether violations were occurring.[70]

Unlike the liberalized standing approach, the guardianship approach would secure an effective voice for the environment even where federal administrative action and public-lands and waters were not involved. It would also allay one of the fears courts—such as the Ninth Circuit—have about the extended standing concept: if any ad hoc group can spring up overnight, invoke some "right" as universally claimable as the esthetic and recreational interests of its members and thereby get into court, how can a flood of litigation be prevented?[71] If an ad hoc committee loses a suit brought *sub nom.* Committee to Preserve our Trees, what happens when its very same members reorganize two years later and sue *sub nom.* the Massapequa Sylvan Protection League? Is the new group bound by res judicata? Class action law may be capable of ameliorating some of the more obvious problems. But even so, court economy might be better served by simply designating the guardian de jure representative of the natural object, with rights of

---

70. These sections create a criminal liability. No civil action lies to enforce it; criminal statutes can only be enforced by the government. A qui tam action lies only when expressly or impliedly authorized by statute to enforce a penalty by civil action, not a criminal fine.
324 F. Supp. 412, 415-16 (N.D., M.D. & S.D. Ala. 1970). Other *qui tam* actions brought by the Bass Angler Sportsman Society have been similarly unsuccessful. *See* Bass Anglers Sportsman Soc'y of America v. Scholze Tannery, 329 F. Supp. 339 (E.D. Tenn. 1971); Bass Anglers Sportsman's Soc'y of America v. United States Plywood-Champion Papers, Inc., 324 F. Supp. 302 (S.D. Tex. 1971).

71. Concern over an anticipated flood of litigation initiated by environmental organizations is evident in Judge Trask's opinion in Alameda Conservation Ass'n v. California, 437 F.2d 1087 (9th Cir.), *cert. denied*, Leslie Salt Co. v. Alameda Conservation Ass'n, 402 U.S. 908 (1971), where a non-profit corporation having as a primary purpose protection of the public's interest in San Francisco Bay was denied standing to seek an injunction prohibiting a land exchange that would allegedly destroy wildlife, fisheries and the Bay's unique flushing characteristics:

Standing is not established by suit initiated by this association simply because it has as one of its purposes the protection of the "public interest" in the waters of the San Francisco Bay. However well intentioned the members may be, they may not by uniting create for themselves a super-administrative agency or a *parens patriae* official status with the capability of over-seeing and of challenging the action of the appointed and elected officials of the state government. Although recent decisions have considerably broadened the concept of standing, we do not find that they go this far. [Citation.]
Were it otherwise the various clubs, political, economic and social now or yet to be organized, could wreak havoc with the administration of government, both federal and state. There are other forums where their voices and their views may be effectively presented, but to have standing to submit a "case or controversy" to a federal court, something more must be shown.
437 F.2d at 1090.

discretionary intervention by others, but with the understanding that the natural object is "bound" by an adverse judgment.[72] The guardian concept, too, would provide the endangered natural object with what the trustee in bankruptcy provides the endangered corporation: a continuous supervision over a period of time, with a consequent deeper understanding of a broad range of the ward's problems, not just the problems present in one particular piece of litigation. It would thus assure the courts that the plaintiff has the expertise and genuine adversity in pressing a claim which are the prerequisites of a true "case or controversy."

The guardianship approach, however, is apt to raise two objections, neither of which seems to me to have much force. The first is that a committee or guardian could not judge the needs of the river or forest in its charge; indeed, the very concept of "needs," it might be said, could be used here only in the most metaphorical way. The second objection is that such a system would not be much different from what we now have: is not the Department of Interior already such a guardian for public lands, and do not most states have legislation empowering their attorneys general to seek relief—in a sort of *parens patriae* way— for such injuries as a guardian might concern himself with?

As for the first objection, natural objects *can* communicate their wants (needs) to us, and in ways that are not terribly ambiguous. I am sure I can judge with more certainty and meaningfulness whether and when my lawn wants (needs) water, than the Attorney General can judge whether and when the United States wants (needs) to take an appeal from an adverse judgment by a lower court. The lawn tells me that it wants water by a certain dryness of the blades and soil—immediately obvious to the touch—the appearance of bald spots, yellowing, and a lack of springiness after being walked on; how does "the United States" communicate to the Attorney General? For similar reasons, the guardian-attorney for a smog-endangered stand of pines could venture with more confidence that his client wants the smog stopped, than the directors of a corporation can assert that "the corporation" wants dividends declared. We make decisions on behalf of, and in the purported interests of, others every day; these "others" are often creatures whose wants are far less verifiable, and even far more metaphysical in conception, than the wants of rivers, trees, and land.[73]

---

72. *See* note 49 *supra.*
73. Here, too, we are dogged by the ontological problem discussed in note 26 *supra.* It is easier to say that the smog-endangered stand of pines "wants" the smog stopped

As for the second objection, one can indeed find evidence that the Department of Interior was conceived as a sort of guardian of the public lands.[74] But there are two points to keep in mind. First, insofar as the Department already is an adequate guardian it is only with respect to the federal public lands as per Article IV, section 3 of the Constitution.[75] Its guardianship includes neither local public lands nor private lands. Second, to judge from the environmentalist literature and from the cases environmental action groups have been bringing, the Department is itself one of the bogeys of the environmental movement. (One thinks of the uneasy peace between the Indians and the Bureau of Indian Affairs.) Whether the various charges be right or wrong, one cannot help but observe that the Department has been charged with several institutional goals (never an easy burden), and is currently looked to for action by quite a variety of interest groups, only one of which is the environmentalists. In this context, a guardian outside the institution becomes especially valuable. Besides, what a person wants, fully to secure his rights, is the ability to retain independent counsel even when, and perhaps especially when, the government is acting "for him" in a beneficent way. I have no reason to doubt, for example, that the Social Security System is being managed "for me"; but I would not want to abdicate my right to challenge its actions as they affect me, should the need arise.[76] I would not ask more trust of national forests, vis-à-vis the Department of Interior. The same considerations apply in the instance of local agencies, such as regional water pollution boards, whose members' expertise in pollution matters is often all too credible.[77]

The objection regarding the availability of attorneys-general as

---

(assuming that to be a jurally significant entity) then it is to venture that the mountain, or the planet earth, or the cosmos, is concerned about whether the pines stand or fall. The more encompassing the entity of concern, the less certain we can be in venturing judgments as to the "wants" of any particular substance, quality, or species within the universe. Does the cosmos care if we humans persist or not? "Heaven and earth . . . regard all things as insignificant, as though they were playthings made of straw." LAO-TZU, TAO TEH KING 13 (D. Goddard transl. 1919).

74. *See* Knight v. United States Land Ass'n, 142 U.S. 161, 181 (1891).

75. Clause 2 gives Congress the power "to dispose of and make all needful Rules and Regulations respecting the Territory or other Property belonging to the United States."

76. *See* Flemming v. Nestor, 363 U.S. 603 (1960).

77. *See* the L. A. Times editorial *Water: Public vs. Polluters* criticizing:

. . . the ridiculous built-in conflict of interests on Regional Water Quality Control Board. By law, five of the seven seats are given to spokesmen for industrial, governmental, agricultural or utility users. Only one representative of the public at large is authorized, along with a delegate from fish and game interests.

Feb. 12, 1969, Part II, at 8, cols. 1-2.

protectors of the environment within the existing structure is somewhat the same. Their statutory powers are limited and sometimes unclear. As political creatures, they must exercise the discretion they have with an eye toward advancing and reconciling a broad variety of important social goals, from preserving morality to increasing their jurisdiction's tax base. The present state of our environment, and the history of cautious application and development of environmental protection laws long on the books,[78] testifies that the burdens of an attorney-general's broad responsibility have apparently not left much manpower for the protection of nature. (*Cf. Bass Anglers*, above.) No doubt, strengthening interest in the environment will increase the zest of public attorneys even where, as will often be the case, well-represented corporate polluters are the quarry. Indeed, the United States Attorney General has stepped up anti-pollution activity, and ought to be further encouraged in this direction.[79] The statutory powers of the attorneys-general should be enlarged, and they should be armed with criminal penalties made at least commensurate with the likely economic benefits of violating the law.[80] On the other hand, one cannot ignore the fact that there is increased pressure on public law-enforcement offices to give more attention to a host of other problems, from crime "on the streets" (why don't we say "in the rivers"?) to consumerism and school bussing. If the environment is not to get lost in the shuffle, we would do well, I think, to adopt the guardianship approach as an additional safeguard, conceptualizing major natural objects as holders of their own rights, raisable by the court-appointed guardian.

### Toward Recognition of its Own Injuries

As far as adjudicating the merits of a controversy is concerned, there is also a good case to be made for taking into account harm to the environment—in its own right. As indicated above, the traditional way of deciding whether to issue injunctions in law suits affecting the environment, at least where communal property is involved, has been to strike some sort of balance regarding the economic hardships *on human*

---

78. The Federal Refuse Act is over 70 years old. Refuse Act of 1899, 33 U.S.C. § 407 (1970).

79. *See* Hall, *Refuse Act of 1899 and the Permit Program*, 1 NAT'L RES. DEFENSE COUNCIL NEWSLETTER i (1971).

80. To be effective as a deterrent, the sanction ought to be high enough to bring about an internal reorganization of the corporate structure which minimizes the chances of future violations. Because the corporation is not necessarily a profit-maximizing "rationally economic man," there is no reason to believe that setting the fine as high as—but no higher than—anticipated profits from the violation of the law, will bring the illegal behavior to an end.

*beings.* Even recently, Mr. Justice Douglas, our jurist most closely associated with conservation sympathies in his private life, was deciding the propriety of a new dam on the basis of, among other things, anticipated lost profits from fish catches, some $12,000,000 annually.[81] Although he decided to delay the project pending further findings, the reasoning seems unnecessarily incomplete and compromising. Why should the environment be of importance only indirectly, as lost profits to someone else? Why not throw into the balance the cost *to the environment?*

The argument for "personifying" the environment, from the point of damage calculations, can best be demonstrated from the welfare economics position. Every well-working legal-economic system should be so structured as to confront each of us with the full costs that our activities are imposing on society.[82] Ideally, a paper-mill, in deciding what to produce—and where, and by what methods—ought to be forced to take into account not only the lumber, acid and labor that its production "takes" from other uses in the society, but also what costs alternative production plans will impose on society through pollution. The legal system, through the law of contracts and the criminal law, for example, makes the mill confront the costs of the first group of demands. When, for example, the company's purchasing agent orders 1000 drums of acid from the Z Company, the Z Company can bind the mill to pay for them, and thereby reimburse the society for what the mill is removing from alternative uses.

Unfortunately, so far as the pollution costs are concerned, the allocative ideal begins to break down, because the traditional legal institutions have a more difficult time "catching" and confronting us with the full social costs of our activities. In the lakeside mill example, major riparian interests might bring an action, forcing a court to weigh *their* aggregate losses against the costs to the mill of installing the

---

81. Udall v. FPC, 387 U.S. 428, 437 n.6 (1967). *See also* Holmes, J. in New Jersey v. New York, 283 U.S. 336, 342 (1931): "A river is more than an amenity, it is a treasure. It offers a necessity of life that must be rationed among those who have power over it."

82. To simplify the description, I am using here an ordinary language sense of causality, *i.e.,* assuming that the pollution causes harm to the river. As Professor Coase has pointed out in *The Problem of Social Cost,* 3 J. LAW & ECON. 1 (1960), harm-causing can be viewed as a reciprocal problem, *i.e.,* in the terms of the text, the mill wants to harm the river, and the river—if we assume it "wants" to maintain its present environmental quality—"wants" to harm the mill. Coase rightly points out that at least in theory (if we had the data) we ought to be comparing the alternative social product of different social arrangements, and not simply imposing full costs on the party who would popularly be identified as the harm-causer.

anti-pollution device. But many other interests—and I am speaking for the moment of recognized homocentric interests—are too fragmented and perhaps "too remote" causally to warrant securing representation and pressing for recovery: the people who own summer homes and motels, the man who sells fishing tackle and bait, the man who rents rowboats. There is no reason not to allow the lake to prove damages to them as the prima facie measure of damages to it. *By doing so, we in effect make the natural object, through its guardian, a jural entity competent to gather up these fragmented and otherwise unrepresented damage claims, and press them before the court even where, for legal or practical reasons, they are not going to be pressed by traditional class action plaintiffs.*[83] Indeed, one way—the homocentric way—to view what I am proposing so far, is to view the guardian of the natural object as the guardian of unborn generations, as well as of the otherwise unrepresented, but distantly injured, contemporary humans.[84] By making the lake itself the focus of these damages, and "incorporating" it so to speak, the legal system can effectively take proof upon, and confront the mill with, a larger and more representative measure of the damages its pollution causes.

So far, I do not suppose that my economist friends (unremittent human chauvanists, every one of them!) will have any large quarrel in principle with the concept. Many will view it as a *trompe l'oeil* that comes down, at best, to effectuate the goals of the paragon class action, or the paragon water pollution control district. Where we are apt to part company is here—I propose going beyond gathering up the loose ends of what most people would presently recognize as economically valid damages. The guardian would urge before the court injuries not presently cognizable—the death of eagles and inedible crabs, the suffering of sea lions, the loss from the face of the earth of species of commercially valueless birds, the disappearance of a wilderness area. One might, of course, speak of the damages involved as "damages" to us

---

83. I am assuming that one of the considerations that goes into a judgment of "remoteness" is a desire to discourage burdensome amounts of petty litigation. This is one of the reasons why a court would be inclined to say—to use the example in the text —that the man who sells fishing tackle and bait has not been "proximately" injured by the polluter. Using proximate cause in this manner, the courts can protect themselves from a flood of litigation. But once the guardian were in court anyway, this consideration would not obtain as strongly, and courts might be more inclined to allow proof on the damages to remotely injured humans (although the proof itself is an added burden of sorts).

84. *Cf.* Golding, *Ethical Issues in Biological Engineering*, 15 U.C.L.A.L. REV. 443, 451-63 (1968).

humans, and indeed, the widespread growth of environmental groups shows that human beings do feel these losses. But they are not, at present, economically measurable losses: how can they have a monetary value for the guardian to prove in court?

The answer for me is simple. Wherever it carves out "property" rights, the legal system is engaged in the process of *creating* monetary worth. One's literary works would have minimal monetary value if anyone could copy them at will. Their economic value to the author is a product of the law of copyright; the person who copies a copy-righted book has to bear a cost to the copyright-holder because the law says he must. Similarly, it is through the law of torts that we have made a "right" of—and guaranteed an economically meaningful value to— privacy. (The value we place on gold—a yellow inanimate dirt—is not simply a function of supply and demand—wilderness areas are scarce and pretty too—, but results from the actions of the legal systems of the world, which have institutionalized that value; they have even done a remarkable job of stabilizing the price). I am proposing we do the same with eagles and wilderness areas as we do with copyrighted works, patented inventions, and privacy: *make* the violation of rights in them to be a cost by declaring the "pirating" of them to be the invasion of a property interest.[85] If we do so, the net social costs the polluter would be confronted with would include not only the extended homocentric costs of his pollution (explained above) but also costs to the environment *per se.*

How, though, would these costs be calculated? When we protect an invention, we can at least speak of a fair market value for it, by reference to which damages can be computed. But the lost environmental "values" of which we are now speaking are by definition over and above those that the market is prepared to bid for: they are priceless.

One possible measure of damages, suggested earlier, would be the cost of making the environment whole, just as, when a man is injured in an automobile accident, we impose upon the responsible party the injured man's medical expenses. Comparable expenses to a polluted river would be the costs of dredging, restocking with fish, and so forth. It is on the basis of such costs as these, I assume, that we get the figure of $1 billion as the cost of saving Lake Erie.[86] As an ideal, I think this

---

85. Of course, in the instance of copyright and patent protection, the creation of the "property right" can be more directly justified on homocentric grounds.

86. *See* Schrag, *Life on a Dying Lake,* in THE POLITICS OF NEGLECT 167, at 173 (R. Meek & J. Straayer eds. 1971).

is a good guide applicable in many environmental situations. It is by no means free from difficulties, however.

One problem with computing damages on the basis of making the environment whole is that, if understood most literally, it is tantamount to asking for a "freeze" on environmental quality, even at the costs (and there will be costs) of preserving "useless" objects.[87] Such a "freeze" is not inconceivable to me as a general goal, especially considering that, even by the most immediately discernible homocentric interests, in so many areas we ought to be cleaning up and not merely preserving the environmental status quo. In fact, there is presently strong sentiment in the Congress for a total elimination of all river pollutants by 1985,[88] notwithstanding that such a decision would impose quite large direct and indirect costs on us all. Here one is inclined to recall the instructions of Judge Hays, in remanding Consolidated Edison's Storm King application to the Federal Power Commission in *Scenic Hudson*:

> The Commission's renewed proceedings must include as a basic concern the preservation of natural beauty and of natural historic shrines, keeping in mind that, in our affluent society, the cost of a project is only one of several factors to be considered.[89]

Nevertheless, whatever the merits of such a goal in principle, there are many cases in which the social price tag of putting it into effect are going to seem too high to accept. Consider, for example, an oceanside nuclear generator that could produce low cost electricity for a million homes at a savings of $1 a year per home, spare us the air pollution that comes of burning fossil fuels, but which through a slight heating effect threatened to kill off a rare species of temperature-sensitive sea urchins; suppose further that technological improvements adequate to reduce the temperature to present environmental quality would expend the entire one million dollars in anticipated fuel savings. Are we prepared to tax ourselves $1,000,000 a year on behalf of the sea

---

87. One ought to observe, too, that in terms of real effect on marginal welfare, the poor quite possibly will bear the brunt of the compromises. They may lack the wherewithal to get out to the countryside—and probably want an increase in material goods more acutely than those who now have riches.

88. On November 2, 1971, the Senate, by a vote of 86-0, passed and sent to the House the proposed Federal Water Pollution Control Act Amendments of 1971, 117 CONG. REC. S17464 (daily ed. Nov. 2, 1971). Sections 101(a) and (a)(1) of the bill declare it to be "national policy that, consistent with the provisions of this Act—(1) the discharge of pollutants into the navigable waters be eliminated by 1985." S.2770, 92d Cong., 1st Sess., 117 CONG. REC. S17464 (daily ed. Nov. 2, 1971).

89. 354 F.2d 608, 624 (2d Cir. 1965).

urchins? In comparable problems under the present law of damages, we work out practicable compromises by abandoning restoration costs and calling upon fair market value. For example, if an automobile is so severely damaged that the cost of bringing the car to its original state by repair is greater than the fair market value, we would allow the responsible tortfeasor to pay the fair market value only. Or if a human being suffers the loss of an arm (as we might conceive of the ocean having irreparably lost the sea urchins), we can fall back on the capitalization of reduced earning power (and pain and suffering) to measure the damages. But what is the fair market value of sea urchins? How can we capitalize their loss to the ocean, independent of any commercial value they may have to someone else?

One answer is that the problem can sometimes be sidestepped quite satisfactorily. In the sea urchin example, one compromise solution would be to impose on the nuclear generator the costs of making the ocean whole somewhere else, in some other way, *e.g.*, reestablishing a sea urchin colony elsewhere, or making a somehow comparable contribution.[90] In the debate over the laying of the trans-Alaskan pipeline, the builders are apparently prepared to meet conservationists' objections half-way by re-establishing wildlife away from the pipeline, so far as is feasible.[91]

But even if damage calculations have to be made, one ought to recognize that the measurement of damages is rarely a simple report of economic facts about "the market," whether we are valuing the loss of a foot, a foetus, or a work of fine art. Decisions of this sort are always hard, but not impossible. We have increasingly taken (human) pain and suffering into account in reckoning damages, not because we think we can ascertain them as objective "facts" about the universe, but because, even in view of all the room for disagreement, we come up with a better society by making rude estimates of them than by ignoring them.[92] We can make such estimates in regard to environmental losses

90. Again, there is a problem involving what we conceive to be the injured entity. *See* notes 26, 73 *supra*.

91. N.Y. Times, Jan. 14, 1971, § 1, col. 2, and at 74, col. 7.

92. Courts have not been reluctant to award damages for the destruction of heirlooms, literary manuscripts or other property having no ascertainable market value. In Willard v. Valley Gas Fuel Co., 171 Cal. 9, 151 Pac. 286 (1915), it was held that the measure of damages for the negligent destruction of a rare old book written by one of plaintiff's ancestors was the amount which would compensate the owner for all detriment including sentimental loss proximately caused by such destruction. The court, at 171 Cal. 15, 151 Pac. 289, quoted approvingly from Southern Express Co. v. Owens. 146 Ala. 412, 426, 41 S. 752, 755 (1906):

fully aware that what we are really doing is making implicit normative judgments (as with pain and suffering)—laying down rules as to what the society is going to "value" rather than reporting market evaluations. In making such normative estimates decision-makers would not go wrong if they estimated on the "high side," putting the burden of trimming the figure down on the immediate human interests present. All burdens of proof should reflect common experience; our experience in environmental matters has been a continual discovery that our acts have caused more long-range damage than we were able to appreciate at the outset.

To what extent the decision-maker should factor in costs such as the pain and suffering of animals and other sentient natural objects, I cannot say; although I am prepared to do so in principle.[93] Given the conjectural nature of the "estimates" in all events, and the roughness of the "balance of conveniences" procedure where that is involved, the

---

Ordinarily, where property has a market value that can be shown, such value is the criterion by which actual damages for its destruction or loss may be fixed. But it may be that property destroyed or lost has no market value. In such state of the case, while it may be that no rule which will be absolutely certain to do justice between the parties can be laid down, it does not follow from this, nor is it the law, that the plaintiff must be turned out of court with nominal damages merely. Where the article or thing is so unusual in its character that market value cannot be predicated of it, its value, or plaintiff's damages, must be ascertained in some other rational way and from such elements as are attainable.

Similarly, courts award damages in wrongful death actions despite the impossibility of precisely appraising the damages in such cases. In affirming a judgment in favor of the administrator of the estate of a child killed by defendant's automobile, the Oregon Supreme Court, in Lane v. Hatfield, 173 Or. 79, 88-89, 143 P.2d 230, 234 (1943), acknowledged the speculative nature of the measure of damages:

No one knows or can know when, if at all, a seven year old girl will attain her majority, for her marriage may take place before she has become twenty-one years of age. . . . Moreover, there is much uncertainty with respect to the length of time anyone may live. A similar uncertainty veils the future of a minor's earning capacity or habit of saving. Illness or a non-fatal accident may reduce an otherwise valuable and lucrative life to a burden and liability.

The rule, that the measure of recovery by a personal representative for the wrongful death of his decedent is the value of the life of such decedent, if he had not come to such an untimely end, has been termed vague, uncertain and speculative if not, conjectural. It is, however, the best that judicial wisdom has been able to formulate.

93. It is not easy to dismiss the idea of "lower" life having consciousness and feeling pain, especially since it is so difficult to know what these terms mean even as applied to humans. *See* Austin, *Other Minds*, in *Logic and Language* 342 (S. Flew ed. 1965); Schopenhauer, *On the Will in Nature*, in Two Essays by Arthur Schopenhauer 193, 281-304 (1889). Some experiments on plant sensitivity—of varying degrees of extravagance in their claims—include Lawrence, *Plants Have Feelings, Too . . .* , Organic Gardening & Farming 64 (April 1971); Woodlief, Royster & Huang, *Effect of Random Noise on Plant Growth*, 46 J. Acoustical Soc. Am. 481 (1969); Backster, *Evidence of a Primary Perception in Plant Life*, 10 Int'l J. Parapsychology 250 (1968).

practice would be of more interest from the socio-psychic point of view, discussed below, than from the legal-operational.

### Toward Being a Beneficiary in its Own Right

As suggested above, one reason for making the environment itself the beneficiary of a judgment is to prevent it from being "sold out" in a negotiation among private litigants who agree not to enforce rights that have been established among themselves.[94] Protection from this will be advanced by making the natural object a party to an injunctive settlement. Even more importantly, we should make it a beneficiary of money awards. If, in making the balance requisite to issuing an injunction, a court decides *not* to enjoin a lake polluter who is causing injury to the extent of $50,000 annually, then the owners and the lake ought both to be awarded damages. The natural object's portion could be put into a trust fund to be administered by the object's guardian, as per the guardianship recommendation set forth above. So far as the damages are proved, as suggested in the previous section, by allowing the natural object to cumulate damages to others as prima facie evidence of damages to it, there will, of course, be problems of distribution. But even if the object is simply construed as representing a class of plaintiffs under the applicable civil rules,[95] there is often likely to be a sizeable amount of recovery attributable to members of the class who will not put in a claim for distribution (because their pro rata share would be so small, or because of their interest in the environment). Not only should damages go into these funds, but where criminal fines are applied (as against water polluters) it seems to me that the monies (less prosecutorial expenses, perhaps) ought sensibly to go to the fund rather than to the general treasuries. Guardians fees, including legal fees, would then come out of this fund. More importantly, the fund would be available to preserve the natural object as close as possible to its condition at the time the environment was made a rights-holder.[96]

The idea of assessing damages as best we can and placing them in a trust fund is far more realistic than a hope that a total "freeze" can be put on the environmental status quo. Nature is a continuous theatre in which things and species (eventually man) are destined to enter and

---

94. *See* note 39 *supra*, and Coase, note 82 *supra*.

95. *See* FED. R. CIV. P. 23 and note 49 *supra*.

96. This is an ideal, of course—like the ideal that no human being ought to interfere with any other human being. *See* Dyke, *Freedom, Consent and the Costs of Interaction*, and Stone, *Comment*, in IS LAW DEAD? 134-67 (E. Rostow ed. 1971). Some damages would inevitably be *damnum absque injuria*. *See* note 93 *supra*.

exit.[97] In the meantime, co-existence of man and his environment means that *each* is going to have to compromise for the better of both. Some pollution of streams, for example, will probably be inevitable for some time. Instead of setting an unrealizable goal of enjoining absolutely the discharge of all such pollutants, the trust fund concept would (a) help assure that pollution would occur only in those instances where the social need for the pollutant's product (via his present method of production) was so high as to enable the polluter to cover *all* homocentric costs, plus some estimated costs to the environment *per se*, and (b) would be a corpus for preserving monies, if necessary, while the technology developed to a point where repairing the damaged portion of the environment was feasible. Such a fund might even finance the requisite research and development.

(Incidentally, if "rights" are to be granted to the environment, then for many of the same reasons it might bear "liabilities" as well—as inanimate objects did anciently.[98] Rivers drown people, and flood over and destroy crops; forests burn, setting fire to contiguous communities. Where trust funds had been established, they could be available for the satisfaction of judgments *against* the environment, making it bear the costs of some of the harms it imposes on other right holders. In effect, we would be narrowing the claim of Acts of God. The ontological problem would be troublesome here, however; when the Nile overflows, is it the "responsibility" of the river? the mountains? the snow? the hydrologic cycle?[99])

## Toward Rights in Substance

So far we have been looking at the characteristics of being a *holder of rights*, and exploring some of the implications that making the environment a holder of rights would entail. Natural objects would have

---

97. The inevitability of some form of evolution is not inconsistent with the establishment of a legal system that attempts to interfere with or ameliorate the process: is the same not true of the human law we now have, *e.g.*, the laws against murder?

98. Holmes, *Early Forms of Liability*, in THE COMMON LAW (1881), discusses the liability of animals and inanimate objects in early Greek, early Roman and some later law. Alfred's Laws (A.D. 871-901) provided, for example, that a tree by which a man was killed should "be given to the kindred, and let them have it off the land within 30 nights." *Id.* at 19. In Edward I's time, if a man fell from a tree the tree was deodand. *Id.* at 24. Perhaps the liability of non-human matter is, in the history of things, part of a paranoid, defensive phase in man's development; as humans become more abundant, both from the point of material wealth and internally, they may be willing to allow an advance to the stage where non-human matter has rights.

99. *See* note 26 *supra*. In the event that a person built his house near the edge of a river that flooded, would "assumption of the risk" be available on the river's behalf?

standing in their own right, through a guardian; damage to and through them would be ascertained and considered as an independent factor; and they would be the beneficiaries of legal awards. But these considerations only give us the skeleton of what a meaningful rights-holding would involve. To flesh out the "rights" of the environment demands that we provide it with a significant body of rights for it to invoke when it gets to court.

In this regard, the lawyer is constantly aware that a right is not, as the layman may think, some strange substance that one either has or has not. One's life, one's right to vote, one's property, can all be taken away. But those who would infringe on them must go through certain procedures to do so; these procedures are a measure of what we value as a society. Some of the most important questions of "right" thus turn into questions of degree: how much review, and of which sort, will which agencies of state accord us when we claim our "right" is being infringed?

We do not have an absolute right either to our lives or to our driver's licenses. But we have a greater right to our lives because, if even the state wants to deprive us of that "right," there are authoritative bodies that will demand that the state make a very strong showing before it does so, and it will have to justify its actions before a grand jury, petit jury (convincing them "beyond a reasonable doubt"), sentencing jury, and, most likely, levels of appellate courts. The carving out of students "rights" to their education is being made up of this sort of procedural fabric. No one, I think, is maintaining that in no circumstances ought a student to be expelled from school. The battle for student "rights" involves shifting the answers to questions like: before a student is expelled, does he have to be given a hearing; does he have to have prior notice of the hearing, and notice of charges; may he bring counsel, (need the state provide counsel if he cannot?); need there be a transcript; need the school carry the burden of proving the charges; may he confront witnesses; if he is expelled, can he get review by a civil court; if he can get such review, need the school show its actions were "reasonable," or merely "not unreasonable," and so forth?[100]

In this vein, to bring the environment into the society as a rights-holder would not stand it on a better footing than the rest of us mere mortals, who every day suffer injuries that are *damnum absque injuria*.

---

100. *See* Dixon v. Alabama State Bd. of Educ., 294 F.2d 150 (5th Cir.), *cert. denied*, 368 U.S. 930 (1961); Comment, *Private Government on the Campus—Judicial Review of University Expulsions*, 72 YALE L.J. 1362 (1963).

What the environment must look for is that its interests be taken into account in subtler, more procedural ways.

The National Environmental Policy Act is a splendid example of this sort of rights-making through the elaboration of procedural safeguards. Among its many provisions, it establishes that every federal agency must:

> (C) include in every recommendation or report on proposals for legislation and other major Federal actions significantly affecting the quality of the human environment, a detailed statement by the responsible official on—
>
> > (i) the environmental impact of the proposed action,
> >
> > (ii) any adverse environmental effects which cannot be avoided should the proposal be implemented,
> >
> > (iii) alternatives to the proposed action,
> >
> > (iv) the relationship between local short-term uses of man's environment and the maintenance and enhancement of long-term productivity, and
> >
> > (v) any irreversible and irretrievable commitments of resources which would be involved in the proposed action should it be implemented.

Prior to making any detailed statement, the responsible Federal official shall consult with and obtain the comments of any Federal agency which has jurisdiction by law or special expertise with respect to any environmental impact involved. Copies of such statement and the comments and views of the appropriate Federal, State, and local agencies, which are authorized to develop and enforce environmental standards, shall be made available to the President, the Council on Environmental Quality and to the public as provided by section 552 of title 5, United States Code, and shall accompany the proposal through the existing agency review processes;

> (D) study, develop, and describe appropriate alternatives to recommended courses of action in any proposal which involves unresolved conflicts concerning alternative uses of available resources;
>
> (E) recognize the worldwide and long-range character of environmental problems and, where consistent with the foreign policy of the United States, lend appropriate support to initiatives,

resolutions, and programs designed to maximize international co-operation in anticipating and preventing a decline in the quality of mankind's environment;

    (F) make available to States, counties, municipalities, institutions, and individuals, advice and information useful in restoring, maintaining, and enhancing the quality of the environment . . . .[101]

These procedural protections have already begun paying off in the courts. For example, it was on the basis of the Federal Power Commission's failure to make adequate inquiry into "alternatives" (as per subsection (iii)) in *Scenic Hudson*, and the Atomic Energy Commission's failure to make adequate findings, apparently as per subsections (i) and (ii), in connection with the Amchitka Island underground test explosion,[102] that Federal Courts delayed the implementation of environment-threatening schemes.

Although this sort of control (remanding a cause to an agency for further findings) may seem to the layman ineffectual, or only a stalling of the inevitable, the lawyer and the systems analyst know that these demands for further findings can make a difference. It may encourage the institution whose actions threaten the environment to really *think about* what it is doing, and that is neither an ineffectual nor a small feat. Indeed, I would extend the principle beyond federal agencies. Much of the environment is threatened not by them, but by private corporations. Surely the constitutional power would not be lacking to mandate that all private corporations whose actions may have significant adverse affect on the environment make findings of the sort now mandated for federal agencies. Further, there should be requirements that these findings and reports be channeled to the Board of Directors; if the directors are not charged with the knowledge of what their corporation is doing to the environment, it will be all too easy for lower level management to prevent such reports from getting to a policy-making level. We might make it grounds for a guardian to enjoin a private corporation's actions if such procedures had not been carried out.

The rights of the environment could be enlarged by borrowing yet another page from the Environmental Protection Act and mandating comparable provisions for "private governments." The Act sets up

---

    101.  National Environmental Policy Act, 92 U.S.C. § 4332 (1970).

    102.  *See* Committee for Nuclear Responsibility Inc. v. Schlesinger, 40 U.S.L.W. 3214 (Nov. 5, 1971) (Douglas, J. dissent to denial of application for injunction in aid of jurisdiction).

within the Executive Office of the President a Council on Environmental Quality "to be conscious of and responsive to the scientific, economic, social, esthetic, and cultural needs of the Nation; and to formulate and recommend national policies to promote the improvement of the quality of the environment."[103] The Council is to become a focal point, within our biggest "corporation"—the State—to gather and evaluate environmental information which it is to pass on to our chief executive officer, the President. Rather than being ineffectual, this may be a highly sophisticated way of steering organizational behavior. Corporations—especially recidivist polluters and land despoilers—should have to establish comparable internal reorganization, *e.g.*, to set up a Vice-President for Ecological Affairs. The author is not offering this suggestion as a cure-all, by any means, but I do not doubt that this sort of control over internal corporate organization would be an effective supplement to the traditional mechanisms of civil suits, licensing, administrative agencies, and fines.[104]

Similarly, courts, in making rulings that may affect the environment, should be compelled to make findings with respect to environmental harm—showing how they calculated it and how heavily it was weighed—even in matters outside the present Environmental Protection Act. This would have at least two important consequences. First, it would shift somewhat the focus of court-room testimony and concern; second, the appellate courts, through their review and reversals for "insufficient findings," would give content to, and build up a body of, environmental rights, much as content and body has been given, over the years, to terms like "Due Process of Law."

Beyond these procedural safeguards, would there be any rights of the environment that might be deemed "absolute," at least to the extent of, say, Free Speech? Here, the doctrine of irreparable injury comes to mind. There has long been equitable support for an attorney-general's enjoining injury to communal property if he can prove it to be "irreparable." In other words, while repairable damage to the environment

---

103. 42 U.S.C. § 4342 (1970).

104. As an indication of what lower-level management is apt to do, *see* Ehrenreich & Ehrenreich, *Conscience of a Steel Worker*, 213 THE NATION 268 (1971). One steel company's "major concession [toward obedience to the 1899 Refuse Act, note 78 *supra*] was to order the workers to confine oil dumping to the night shift. 'During the day the Coast Guard patrols. But at night, the water's black, the oil's black; no one can tell.'" An effective corporation law would assure that the internal information channels within a corporation were capable of forcing such matters to the attention of high-level officials. Even then, there is no guarantee that the law will be obeyed—but we may have improved the odds.

might be balanced and weighed, irreparable damage could be enjoined absolutely. There are several reasons why this doctrine has not been used effectively (witness Lake Erie).[105] Undoubtedly, political pressures (in the broadest sense) have had an influence. So, too, has the failure of all of us to understand just how delicate the environmental balance is; this failure has made us unaware of how early "irreparable" injury might be occurring, and, if aware, unable to prove it in court. But most important I think, is that the doctrine simply is not practical as a rule of universal application. For one thing, there are too many cases like the sea urchin example above, where the marginal costs of abating the damage seem too clearly to exceed the marginal benefits, even if the damage to the environment itself is liberally estimated. For another, there is a large problem in how one defines "irreparable." Certainly the great bulk of the environment in civilized parts of the world has been injured "irreparably" in the sense of "irreversably"; we are not likely to return it to its medieval quality. Despite the scientific ring to the term, judgments concerning "irreparable injury" are going to have to subsume questions both of degree of damage and of value—to all of "us" including the environment, i.e., to "spaceship earth"—of the damaged object. Thus, if we are going to revitalize the "irreparable damages" doctrine, and expect it to be taken seriously, we have to recognize that what will be said to constitute "irreparable damage" to the ionosphere, because of its importance to all life, or to the Grand Canyon, because of its uniqueness, is going to rest upon normative judgments that ought to be made explicit.

This suggests that some (relatively) absolute rights be defined for the environment by setting up a constitutional list of "preferred objects," just as some of our Justices feel there are "preferred rights" where humans are concerned.[106] Any threatened injury to these most jealously-to-be-protected objects should be reviewed with the highest level of scrutiny at all levels of government, including our "counter-majoritarian" branch, the court system. Their "Constitutional rights" should be implemented, legislatively and administratively, by, e.g., the setting of environmental quality standards.

I do not doubt that other senses in which the environment might

---

105. In the case of Lake Erie, in addition to the considerations that follow in the text, there were possibly additional factors such as that no one polluter's acts could be characterized as inflicting irreparable injury.

106. See for example Justice Reed's opinion for the Court in Kovacs v. Cooper, 336 U.S. 77 (1949) (but see Mr. Justice Frankfurter's concurring opinion, 336 U.S. at 89-96), and United States v. Carolene Products, 304 U.S. 144, 152 n.4 (1938).

have rights will come to mind, and, as I explain more fully below, would be more apt to come to mind if only we should speak in terms of their having rights, albeit vaguely at first. "Rights" might well lie in unanticipated areas. It would seem, for example, that Chief Justice Warren was only stating the obvious when he observed in *Reynolds v. Sims* that "legislators represent people, not trees or acres." Yet, could not a case be made for a system of apportionment which *did* take into account the wildlife of an area?[107] It strikes me as a poor idea that Alaska should have no more congressmen than Rhode Island primarily *because there are in Alaska all those trees and acres, those waterfalls and forests.*[108] I am not saying anything as silly as that we ought to overrule *Baker v. Carr* and retreat from one man-one vote to a system of one man-or-tree one vote. Nor am I even taking the position that we ought to count each acre, as we once counted each slave, as three-fifths of a man. But I am suggesting that there is nothing unthinkable about, and there might on balance even be a prevailing case to be made for, an electoral apportionment that made some systematic effort to allow for the representative "rights" of non-human life. And if a case can be made for that, which I offer here mainly for purpose of illustration, I suspect that a society that grew concerned enough about the environment to make it a holder of rights would be able to find quite a number of "rights" to have waiting for it when it got to court.

### Do We Really Have to Put it that Way?

At this point, one might well ask whether much of what has been written could not have been expressed without introducing the notion of trees, rivers, and so forth "having rights." One could simply and straightforwardly say, for example, that ($R_1$) "the class of persons competent to challenge the pollution of rivers ought to be extended beyond that of persons who can show an immediate adverse economic impact on themselves," and that ($R_2$), "judges, in weighing competing claims to a wilderness area, ought to think beyond the economic and even esthetic impact on man, and put into the balance a concern for the threatened environment as such." And it is true, indeed, that to say trees and rivers have "rights" is not in itself a stroke of any operational significance—no more than to say "people have rights." To solve any concrete case,

---

107. Note that in the discussion that follows I am referring to legislative apportionment, not voting proper.

108. In point of fact, there is no reason to suppose that an increase of Congressmen for Alaska would be a benefit to the environment; the reality of the political situation might just as likely result in the election of additional Congressmen with closer ties to oil companies and other developers.

one is always forced to more precise and particularized statements, in which the word "right" might just as well be dropped from the elocution.

But this is not the same as to suggest that introducing the notion of the "rights" of trees and rivers would accomplish nothing beyond the introduction of a set of particular rules like ($R_1$) and ($R_2$), above. I think it is quite misleading to say that "*A* has a right to . . ." can be fully explicated in terms of a certain set of specific legal rules, and the manner in which conclusions are drawn from them in a legal system. That is only part of the truth. Introducing the notion of something having a "right" (simply *speaking* that way), brings into the legal system a flexibility and open-endedness that no series of specifically stated legal rules like $R_1, R_2, R_3, . . . R_n$ can capture. Part of the reason is that "right" (and other so-called "legal terms" like "infant," "corporation," "reasonable time") have meaning—vague but forceful—in the ordinary language, and the force of these meanings, inevitably infused with our thought, becomes part of the context against which the "legal language" of our contemporary "legal rules" is interpreted.[109] Consider, for example, the "rules" that govern the question, on whom, and at what stages of litigation, is the burden of proof going to lie? Professor Krier has demonstrated how terribly significant these decisions are in the trial of environmental cases, and yet, also, how much discretion judges have under them.[110] In the case of such vague rules, it is *context*—senses of direction, of value and purpose— that determines how the rules will be understood, every bit as much as their supposed "plain meaning." In a system which spoke of the environment "having legal rights," judges would, I suspect, be inclined to interpret rules such as those of burden of proof far more liberally from the point of the environment. There is, too, the fact that the vocabulary and expressions that are available to us influence and even steer our thought. Consider the effect that was had by introducing into the law terms like "motive," "intent," and "due process." These terms work a subtle shift into the rhetoric of explanation available to judges; with them, new ways of thinking and

---

109. *See* Simpson, *The Analysis of Legal Concepts*, 80 LAW Q. REV. 535 (1964).

110. Krier, *Environmental Litigation and the Burden of Proof*, in LAW AND THE ENVIRONMENT 105 (M. Baldwin & J. Page eds. 1970). *See* Texas East Trans. Corp. v. Wildlife Preserves, 48 N.J. 261, 225 A.2d 130 (1966). There, where a corporation set up to maintain a wildlife preserve resisted condemnation for the construction of plaintiff's pipe line, the court ruled that ". . . the *quantum* of proof required of this defendant to show arbitrariness against it would not be as substantial as that to be assumed by the ordinary property owner who devotes his land to conventional uses." 225 A.2d at 137.

new insights come to be explored and developed.[111] In such fashion, judges who could unabashedly refer to the "legal rights of the environment" would be encouraged to develop a viable body of law—in part simply through the availability and force of the expression. Besides, such a manner of speaking by courts would contribute to popular notions, and a society that spoke of the "legal rights of the environment" would be inclined to legislate more environment-protecting rules by formal enactment.

If my sense of these influences is correct, then a society in which it is stated, however vaguely, that "rivers have legal rights" would evolve a different legal system than one which did not employ that expression, even if the two of them had, at the start, the very same "legal rules" in other respects.

## THE PSYCHIC AND SOCIO-PSYCHIC ASPECTS

There are, as we have seen, a number of developments in the law that may reflect a shift from the view that nature exists *for men*. These range from increasingly favorable procedural rulings for environmental action groups—as regards standing and burden of proof requirements, for example—to the enactment of comprehensive legislation such as the National Environmental Policy Act and the thoughtful Michigan Environmental Protection Act of 1970. Of such developments one may say, however, that it is not the environment *per se* that we are prepared to take into account, but that man's increased awareness of possible long range effects on himself militate in the direction of stopping environmental harm in its incipiency. And this is part of the truth, of course. Even the far-reaching National Environmental Policy Act, in its preambulatory "Declaration of National Environmental Policy," comes out both for "restoring and maintaining environmental quality *to the overall welfare and development of man*" as well as for creating and maintaining "conditions under which *man and nature can exist in productive harmony*."[112] Because the health and well-being of mankind depend upon the health of the environment, these goals will often be so mutually supportive that one can avoid deciding whether our rationale is to advance "us" or a new "us" that includes the environment. For example, consider the Federal Insecticide, Fungicide, and Rodenticide

111. See Stone, *Existential Humanism and the Law*, in EXISTENTIAL HUMANISTIC PSYCHOLOGY 151 (T. Greening ed. 1971).

112. National Environmental Policy Act, 42 U.S.C. §§ 4321-47 (1970).

Act (FIFRA) which insists that, *e.g.*, pesticides, include a warning "adequate to prevent injury to living man and other vertebrate animals, vegetation, and useful invertebrate animals."[113] Such a provision undoubtedly reflects the sensible notion that the protection of humans is best accomplished by preventing dangerous accumulations in the food chain. Its enactment does not necessarily augur far-reaching changes in, nor even call into question, fundamental matters of consciousness.

But the time is already upon us when we may have to consider subordinating some human claims to those of the environment *per se.* Consider, for example, the disputes over protecting wilderness areas from development that would make them accessible to greater numbers of people. I myself feel disingenuous rationalizing the environmental protectionist's position in terms of a utilitarian calculus, even one that takes future generations into account, and plays fast and loose with its definition of "good." Those who favor development have the stronger argument—they at least hold the protectionist to a standstill—from the point of advancing the greatest good of the greatest number of people. And the same is true regarding arguments to preserve useless species of animals, as in the sea urchin hypothetical. One *can* say that we never know what is going to prove useful at some future time. In order to protect ourselves, therefore, we ought to be conservative now in our treatment of nature. I agree. But when conservationists argue this way to the exclusion of other arguments, or find themselves speaking in terms of "recreational interests" so continuously as to play up to, and reinforce, homocentrist perspectives, there is something sad about the spectacle. One feels that the arguments lack even their proponent's convictions. I expect they want to say something less egotistic and more emphatic but the prevailing and sanctioned modes of explanation in our society are not quite ready for it. In this vein, there must have been abolitonists who put their case in terms of getting more work out of the Blacks. Holdsworth says of the early English Jew that while he was "regarded as a species of res nullius . . . [H]e was valuable for his acquisitive capacity; and for that reason the crown took him under its protection."[114] (Even today, businessmen are put in the position of insisting that their decent but probably profitless acts will "help our company's reputation and be good for profits."[115])

---

113. *See* note 65 *supra.*

114. W. HOLDSWORTH, HISTORY OF ENGLISH LAW 45 (5th ed. 1931).

115. Note that it is in no small way the law that imposes this manner of speech on businessmen. *See* Dodge v. Ford Motor Co., 204 Mich. 459, 499-505, 170 N.W. 668, 682-83 (1919) (holding that Henry Ford, as dominant stockholder in Ford Motor Co., could

For my part, I would prefer a frank avowal that even making adjustments for esthetic improvemens, what I am proposing is going to cost "us," *i.e.*, reduce our standard of living as measured in terms of our present values.

Yet, this frankness breeds a frank response—one which I hear from my colleagues and which must occur to many a reader. Insofar as the proposal is not just an elaborate legal fiction, but really comes down in the last analysis to a compromise of *our* interests for *theirs*, why should we adopt it? "What is in it for 'us'?"

This is a question I am prepared to answer, but only after permitting myself some observations about how *odd* the question is. It asks for me to justify my position in the very anthropocentric hedonist terms that I am proposing we modify. One is inclined to respond by a counter: "couldn't you (as a white) raise the same questions about compromising your preferred rights-status with Blacks?"; or "couldn't you (as a man) raise the same question about compromising your preferred rights-status with women?" Such counters, unfortunately, seem no more responsive than the question itself. (They have a nagging ring of "yours too" about them.) What the exchange actually points up is a fundamental problem regarding the nature of philosophical argument. Recall that Socrates, whom we remember as an opponent of hedonistic thought, confutes Thrasymachus by arguing that immorality makes one miserably unhappy! Kant, whose moral philosophy was based upon the categorical imperative ("Woe to him who creeps through the serpent windings of Utilitarianism"[116]) finds himself justifying, *e.g.*, promise keeping and truth telling, on the most prudential—one might almost say, commercial—grounds.[117] This "philosophic irony" (as Professor Engel calls it) may owe to there being something unique about ethical argument.[118] "Ethics cannot be put into words", Wittgenstein puts it; such matters "make themselves manifest."[119] On the other hand, perhaps the truth is that in any argument which aims at persuading a human being to action (on ethical or any other bases), "logic" is only an instru-

---

not withhold dividends in the interests of operating the company "as a semi-eleemosynary institution and not as a business institution").

116. I. KANT, PHILOSOPHY OF LAW 195 (Hastie Transl. 1887).

117. I. KANT, *The Metaphysics of Morality*, in THE PHILOSOPHY OF KANT § 1 at 230-31 (J. Watson transl. 1908).

118. Engel, *Reasons, Morals and Philosophic Irony*, in LANGUAGE AND ILLUMINATION 60 (1969).

119. L. WITTGENSTEIN, TRACTATUS LOGICO-PHILOSOPHICUS §§ 6.421, 6.522 (D. Pears & B. McGuinness transl. 1961).

ment for illuminating positions, at best, and in the last analysis it is psycho-logical appeals to the listener's self-interest that hold sway, however "principled" the rhetoric may be.

With this reservation as to the peculiar task of the argument that follows, let me stress that the strongest case can be made from the perspective of human advantage for conferring rights on the environment. Scientists have been warning of the crises the earth and all humans on it face if we do not change our ways—radically—and these crises make the lost "recreational use" of rivers seem absolutely trivial. The earth's very atmosphere is threatened with frightening possibilities: absorption of sunlight, upon which the entire life cycle depends, may be diminished; the oceans may warm (increasing the "greenhouse effect" of the atmosphere), melting the polar ice caps, and destroying our great coastal cities; the portion of the atmosphere that shields us from dangerous radiation may be destroyed. Testifying before Congress, sea explorer Jacques Cousteau predicted that the oceans (to which we dreamily look to feed our booming populations) are headed toward their own death: "The cycle of life is intricately tied up with the cycle of water . . . the water system has to remain alive if we are to remain alive on earth."[120] We are depleting our energy and our food sources at a rate that takes little account of the needs even of humans now living.

These problems will not be solved easily; they very likely can be solved, if at all, only through a willingness to suspend the rate of increase in the standard of living (by present values) of the earth's "advanced" nations, and by stabilizing the total human population. For some of us this will involve forfeiting material comforts; for others it will involve abandoning the hope someday to obtain comforts long envied. For all of us it will involve giving up the right to have as many offspring as we might wish. Such a program is not impossible of realization, however. Many of our so-called "material comforts" are not only in excess of, but are probably in opposition to, basic biological needs. Further, the "costs" to the advanced nations is not as large as would appear from Gross National Product figures. G.N.P. reflects social gain (of a sort) without discounting for the social *cost* of that gain, *e.g.*, the losses through depletion of resources, pollution, and so forth. As has well been shown, as societies become more and more "advanced," their real marginal gains become less and less for each additional dollar of

---

120. Cousteau, *The Oceans: No Time to Lose*, L.A. Times, Oct. 24, 1971, § (opinion), at 1, col. 4.

G.N.P.[121] Thus, to give up "human progress" would not be as costly as might appear on first blush.

Nonetheless, such far-reaching social changes are going to involve us in a serious reconsideration of our consciousness towards the environment. I say this knowing full well that there is something more than a trifle obscure in the claim: is popular consciousness a meaningful notion, to begin with? If so, what is our present consciousness regarding the environment? Has it been causally responsible for our material state of affairs? Ought we to shift our consciousness (and if so, to what exactly, and on what grounds)? How, if at all, would a shift in consciousness be translated into tangible institutional reform? Not one of these questions can be answered to everyone's satisfactions, certainly not to the author's.

It is commonly being said today, for example, that our present state of affairs—at least in the West—can be traced to the view that Nature is the dominion of Man, and that this attitude, in turn, derives from our religious traditions.

> Whatever the origins, the text is quite clear in Judaism, was absorbed all but unchanged into Christianity, and was inflated in Humanism to become the implicit attitude of Western man to Nature and the environment. Man is exclusively divine, all other creatures and things occupy lower and generally inconsequential stature; man is given dominion over all creatures and things; he is enjoined to subdue the earth. . . . This environment was created by the man who believes that the cosmos is a pyramid erected to support man on its pinnacle, that reality exists only because man can perceive it, that God is made in the image of man, and that the world consists solely of a dialogue between men. Surely this is an infantalism which is unendurable. It is a residue from a past of inconsequence when a few puny men cried of their supremacy to an unhearing and uncaring world. One longs for a psychiatrist who can assure man that his deep seated cultural inferiority is no longer necessary or appropriate. . . . It is not really necessary to destroy nature in order to gain God's favor or even his undivided attention.[122]

Surely this is forcibly put, but it is not entirely convincing as an explanation for how we got to where we are. For one thing, so far as

---

121. *See* J. HARTE & R. SOCOLOW, PATIENT EARTH (1971).

122. McHarg, *Values, Process and Form*, in THE FITNESS OF MAN'S ENVIRONMENT 213-14 (1968).

intellectual influences are to be held responsible for our present state of affairs, one might as fairly turn on Darwin as the Bible. It was, after all, Darwin's views—in part through the prism of Spencer—that gave moral approbation to struggle, conquest, and domination; indeed, by emphasizing man's development as a product of chance happenings, Darwin also had the effect—intended or not—of reducing our awareness of the mutual interdependency of everything in Nature. And besides, as Professor Murphy points out, the spiritual beliefs of the Chinese and Indians "in the unity between man and nature had no greater effect than the contrary beliefs in Europe in producing a balance between man and his environment"; he claims that in China, *tao* notwithstanding, "ruthless deforestation has been continuous."[123] I am under the impression, too, that notwithstanding the vaunted "harmony" between the American Plains Indians and Nature, once they had equipped themselves with rifles their pursuit of the buffalo expanded to fill the technological potential.[124] The fact is, that "consciousness" explanations pass too quickly over the less negative but simpler view of the situation: there are an increasing number of humans, with increasing wants, and there has been an increasing technology to satisfy them at "cost" to the rest of nature. Thus, we ought not to place too much hope that a changed environmental consciousness will in and of itself reverse present trends. Furthermore, societies have long since passed the point where a change in human consciousness on any matter will rescue us from our problems. More then ever before we are in the hands of institutions. These institutions are not "mere legal fictions" moreover—they have wills, minds, purposes, and inertias that are in very important ways their own, *i.e.*, that can transcend and survive changes in the consciousnesses of the individual humans who supposedly comprise them, and whom they supposedly serve. (It is more and more the individual human being, with his consciousness, that is the legal fiction.[125])

---

123. Murphy, *supra* note 27, at 477.

124. On the other hand, the statement in text, and the previous one of Professor Murphy, may be a bit severe. One could as easily claim that Christianity has had no influence on overt human behavior in light of the killings that have been carried out by professed Christians, often in its name. *Feng shui* has, on all accounts I am familiar with, influenced the development of land in China. *See* Freedman, *Geomancy*, 1968 PROCEEDINGS OF THE ROYAL ANTHROPOLOGICAL INSTITUTE OF GREAT BRITAIN AND IRELAND 5; March, *An Appreciation of Chinese Geomancy*, 27 J. ASIAN STUDIES 253 (1968).

125. The legal system does the best it can to maintain the illusion of the reality of the individual human being. Consider, for example, how many constitutional cases, brought in the name of some handy individual, represent a power struggle between institutions—the NAACP and a school board, the Catholic Church and a school board, the ACLU and the Army, and so forth. Are the individual human plaintiffs the real moving causes of these cases—or an afterthought?

For these reasons, it is far too pat to suppose that a western "environmental consciousness" is solely or even primarily responsible for our environmental crisis. On the other hand, it is not so extravagant to claim that it has dulled our resentment and our determination to respond. For this reason, whether we will be able to bring about the requisite institutional and population growth changes depends in part upon effecting a radical shift in our feelings about "our" place in the rest of Nature.

A radical new conception of man's relationship to the rest of nature would not only be a step towards solving the material planetary problems; there are strong reasons for such a changed consciousness from the point of making us far better humans. If we only stop for a moment and look at the underlying human qualities that our present attitudes toward property and nature draw upon and reinforce, we have to be struck by how stultifying of our own personal growth and satisfaction they can become when they take rein of us. Hegel, in "justifying" private property, unwittingly reflects the tone and quality of some of the needs that are played upon:

> A person has as his substantive end the right of putting his will into any and every thing and thereby making it his, because it has no such end in itself and derives its destiny and soul from his will. This is the absolute right of appropriation which man has over all "things."[126]

What is it within us that gives us this need not just to satisfy basic biological wants, but to extend our wills over things, to object-ify them, to make them ours, to manipulate them, to keep them at a psychic distance? Can it all be explained on "rational" bases? Should we not be suspect of such needs within us, cautious as to why we wish to gratify

---

When we recognize that our problems are increasingly institutional, we would see that the solution, if there is one, must involve coming to grips with how the "corporate" (in the broadest sense) entity is directed, and we must alter our views of "property" in the fashion that is needed to regulate organizations successfully. For example, instead of ineffectual, after-the-fact criminal fines we should have more preventive in-plant inspections, notwithstanding the protests of "invasion of [corporate] privacy."

In-plant inspection of production facilities and records is presently allowed only in a narrow range of areas, *e.g.*, in federal law, under the Federal Food, Drug, and Cosmetic Act, 21 U.S.C. § 374 *et seq.* (1970), and provisions for meat inspection, 21 U.S.C. § 608 (1970). Similarly, under local building codes we do not wait for a building to collapse before authoritative sources inquire into the materials and procedures that are being used in the construction; inspectors typically come on site to check the progress at every critical stage. A sensible preventive legal system calls for extending the ambit of industries covered by comparable "privacy invading" systems of inspection.

126. G. HEGEL, HEGEL'S PHILOSOPHY OF RIGHT 41 (T. Knox transl. 1945).

them? When I first read that passage of Hegel, I immediately thought
not only of the emotional contrast with Spinoza, but of the passage in
Carson McCullers' *A Tree, A Rock, A Cloud,* in which an old derelict
has collared a twelve year old boy in a streetcar cafe. The old man asks
whether the boy knows "how love should be begun?"

The old man leaned closer and whispered:

"A tree. A rock. A cloud."
. . .

"The weather was like this in Portland," he said. "At the
time my science was begun. I meditated and I started very
cautious. I would pick up something from the street and take it
home with me. I bought a goldfish and I concentrated on the
goldfish and I loved it. I graduated from one thing to another.
Day by day I was getting this technique. . . .
. . .

. . . "For six years now I have gone around by myself and
built up my science. And now I am a master. Son. I can love anything. No longer do I have to think about it even. I see a street
full of people and a beautiful light comes in me. I watch a bird in
the sky. Or I meet a traveler on the road. Everything, Son. And
anybody. All stranger and all loved! Do you realize what a science
like mine can mean?"[127]

To be able to get away from the view that Nature is a collection of
useful senseless objects is, as McCullers' "madman" suggests, deeply
involved in the development of our abilities to love—or, if that is
putting it too strongly, to be able to reach a heightened awareness of
our own, and others' capacities in their mutual interplay. To do so, we
have to give up some psychic investment in our sense of separateness
and specialness in the universe. And this, in turn, is hard giving indeed,
because it involves us in a flight backwards, into earlier stages of civilization and childhood in which we had to trust (and perhaps fear) our
environment, for we had not then the power to master it. Yet, in doing
so, we—as persons—gradually free ourselves of needs for supportive
illusions. Is not this one of the triumphs for "us" of our giving legal
rights to (or acknowledging the legal rights of) the Blacks and women?[128]

---

127. C. McCullers, The Ballad of the Sad Cafe and Other Stories 150-51 (1958).
128. Consider what Schopenhauer was writing "Of Women," about the time the
Wisconsin Supreme Court was explaining why women were unfit to practice law, note
23 *supra:*

You need only look at the way in which she is formed, to see that woman is
not meant to undergo great labour, whether of the mind or of the body. She pays
the debt of life not by what she does, but by what she suffers; by the pains of

Changes in this sort of consciousness are already developing, for the betterment of the planet and us. There is now federal legislation which "establishes by law"[129]

> the humane ethic that animals should be accorded the basic crea-
> ture comforts of adequate housing, ample food and water, reason-
> able handling, decent sanitation, sufficient ventilation, shelter
> from extremes of weather and temperature, and adequate veteri-
> nary care including the appropriate use of pain-killing drugs. . . .[130]

The Vietnam war has contributed to this movement, as it has to others. Five years ago a Los Angeles mother turned out a poster which read "War is not Healthy for children and other living things."[131] It caught

---

childbearing and care for the child, and by submission to her husband, to whom she should be a patient and cheering companion. The keenest sorrows and joys are not for her, nor is she called upon to display a great deal of strength. The current of her life should be more gentle, peaceful and trivial than man's, without being essentially happier or unhappier.

Women are directly fitted for acting as the nurses and teachers of our early childhood by the fact that they are themselves childish, frivolous and short-sighted; in a word, they are big children all their life long—a kind of intermediate stage between the child and the full-grown man, who is man in the strict sense of the word. . . .

However many disadvantages all this may involve, there is at least this to be said in its favour: that the woman lives more in the present than the man, and that, if the present is at all tolerable, she enjoys it more eagerly. This is the source of that cheerfulness which is peculiar to woman, fitting her to amuse man in his hours of recreation, and, in case of need, to console him when he is borne down by the weight of his cares.

. . . .

. . . [I]t will be found that the fundamental fault of the female character is that it has *no sense of justice*. This is mainly due to the fact, already mentioned, that women are defective in the powers of reasoning and deliberation; but it is also traceable to the position which Nature has assigned to them as the weaker sex. They are dependent, not upon strength, but upon craft; and hence their instinctive capacity for cunning, and their ineradicable tendency to say what is not true. ***For as lions are provided with claws and teeth, and elephants and boars with tusks, bulls with horns, and the cuttle fish with its cloud of inky fluid, so Nature has equipped woman, for her defense and protection, with the arts of dissimulation; and all the power which Nature has conferred upon man in the shape of physical strength and reason, has been bestowed upon women in this form. Hence, dissimulation is innate in woman, and almost as much a quality of the stupid as of the clever. . . .

A. Schopenhauer, *On Women*, in Studies in Pessimism 105-10 (T. B. Saunders transl. 1893).

If a man should write such insensitive drivel today, we would suspect him of being morally and emotionally blind. Will the future judge us otherwise, for venting rather than examining the needs that impel us to treat the environment as a senseless object—to blast to pieces some small atoll to find out whether an atomic weapon works?

129. Of course, the phase one looks toward is a time in which such sentiments need not be prescribed *by law*.

130. The "Purpose of the Legislation" in H.R. Rep. No. 91-1651, 91st Cong., 2d Sess., to the "[Animal] Welfare Act of 1970," 3 U.S. Code Cong. & Admin. News 5103, 5104 (1970). Some of the West Publishing Co. typesetters may not be quite ready for this yet; they printed out the title as "Annual Welfare Act of 1970."

131. *See* McCall's, May, 1971, at 44.

on tremendously—at first, I suspect, because it sounded like another clever protest against the war, *i.e.*, another angle. But as people say such things, and think about them, the possibilities of what they have stumbled upon become manifest—in its suit against the Secretary of Agriculture to cancel the registration of D.D.T., Environmental Defense Fund alleged "biological injury to man and other living things."[132] A few years ago the pollution of streams was thought of only as a problem of smelly, unsightly, unpotable water *i.e.*, to us. Now we are beginning to discover that pollution is a process that destroys wondrously subtle balances of life within the water, and as between the water and its banks. This heightened awareness enlarges our sense of the dangers to us. But it also enlarges our empathy. We are not only developing the scientific capacity, but we are cultivating the personal capacities *within us* to recognize more and more the ways in which nature—like the woman, the Black, the Indian and the Alien—is like us (and we will also become more able realistically to define, confront, live with and admire the ways in which we are all different).[133]

The time may be on hand when these sentiments, and the early stirrings of the law, can be coalesced into a radical new theory or myth —felt as well as intellectualized—of man's relationships to the rest of nature. I do not mean "myth" in a demeaning sense of the term, but in the sense in which, at different times in history, our social "facts" and relationships have been comprehended and integrated by reference to the "myths" that we are co-signers of a social contract, that the Pope is God's agent, and that all men are created equal. Pantheism, Shinto and Tao all have myths to offer. But they are all, each in its own fashion, quaint, primitive and archaic. What is needed is a myth that can fit our growing body of knowledge of geophysics, biology and the cosmos. In

---

132. Environmental Defense Fund, Inc. v. Hardin, 428 F.2d 1093, 1096 (D.C. Cir. 1970). Plaintiffs would thus seem to have urged a broader than literal reading of the statute, 7 U.S.C. § 135(z) (2) (d) (1970), which refers to " . . . living man and other vertebrate animals, vegetation, and useful invertebrate animals."

E.D.F. was joined as petitioners by the National Audubon Society, the Sierra Club, and the West Michigan Environmental Action Council, 428 F.2d at 1094-95 n.5.

133. In the case of the bestowal of rights on other humans, the action also helps the recipient to discover new personal depths and possibilities—new dignity—within himself. I do not want to make much of the possibility that this effect would be relevant in the case of bestowing rights on the environment. But I would not dismiss it out of hand, either. How, after all, do we judge that a man is, say, "flourishing with a new sense of pride and dignity?" What we mean by such statements, and the nature of the evidence upon which we rely in support of them, is quite complex. *See* Austin, note 93 *supra*. A tree treated in a "rightful" manner would respond in a manner that, when described, would sound much like the response of a person accorded "new dignity." *See also* note 93 *supra*.

this vein, I do not think it too remote that we may come to regard the Earth, as some have suggested, as one organism, of which Mankind is a functional part—the mind, perhaps: different from the rest of nature, but different as a man's brain is from his lungs.

Ever since the first Geophysical Year, international scientific studies have shown irrefutably that the Earth as a whole is an organized system of most closely interrelated and indeed interdependent activities. It is, in the broadest sense of the term, an "organism." The so-called life-kingdoms and the many vegetable and animal species are dependent upon each other for survival in a balanced condition of planet-wide existence; and they depend on their environment, conditioned by oceanic and atmospheric currents, and even more by the protective action of the ionosphere and many other factors which have definite rhythms of operation. Mankind is part of this organic planetary whole; and there can be no truly new global society, and perhaps in the present state of affairs no society at all, as long as man will not recognize, accept and enjoy the fact that mankind has a definite function to perform within this planetary organism of which it is an active part.

In order to give a constructive meaning to the activities of human societies all over the globe, these activities—physical and mental—should be understood and given basic value with reference to the wholesome functioning of the entire Earth, and we may add of the entire solar system. This cannot be done (1) if man insists on considering himself an alien Soul compelled to incarnate on this sorrowful planet, and (2) if we can see in the planet, Earth, nothing but a mass of material substances moved by mechanical laws, and in "life" nothing but a chance combination of molecular aggregations.

. . . As I see it, the Earth is only one organized "field" of activities—and so is the *human person*—but these activities take place at various levels, in different "spheres" of being and realms of consciousness. The lithosphere is not the biosphere, and the latter not the . . . ionosphere. The Earth is not *only* a material mass. Consciousness is not only "human"; it exists at animal and vegetable levels, and most likely must be latent, or operating in some form, in the molecule and the atom; and all these diverse and in a sense hierarchical modes of activity and consciousness should be seen integrated in and perhaps transcended by an all-encompassing and "eonic" planetary Consciousness.

. . . .

Mankind's function within the Earth-organism is to extract

from the activities of all other operative systems within this organism the type of consciousness which we call "reflective" or "self"-consciousness—or, we may also say to *mentalize* and give meaning, value, and "name" to all that takes place anywhere within the Earth-field. . . .

This "mentalization" process operates through what we call culture. To each region of, and living condition in the total field of the Earth-organism a definite type of culture inherently corresponds. Each region is the "womb" out of which a specific type of human mentality and culture can and sooner or later will emerge. All these cultures—past, present and future—and their complex interrelationships and interactions are the collective builders of the Mind of humanity; and this means of the *conscious Mind of the Earth*.[134]

As radical as such a consciousness may sound today, all the dominant changes we see about us point in its direction. Consider just the impact of space travel, of world-wide mass media, of increasing scientific discoveries about the interrelatedness of all life processes. Is it any wonder that the term "spaceship earth" has so captured the popular imagination? The problems we have to confront are increasingly the world-wide crises of a global organism: not pollution of a stream, but pollution of the atmosphere and of the ocean. Increasingly, the death that occupies each human's imagination is not his own, but that of the entire life cycle of the planet earth, to which each of us is as but a cell to a body.

To shift from such a lofty fancy as the planetarization of consciousness to the operation of our municipal legal system is to come down to earth hard. Before the forces that are at work, our highest court is but a frail and feeble—a distinctly human—institution. Yet, the Court may be at its best not in its work of handing down decrees, but at the very task that is called for: of summoning up from the human spirit the kindest and most generous and worthy ideas that abound there, giving them shape and reality and legitimacy.[135] Witness the School Desegregation Cases which, more importantly than to integrate the schools (assuming they did), awakened us to moral needs which, when made visible, could not be denied. And so here, too, in the case of the environment, the Supreme Court may find itself in a position to award "rights" in a way that will contribute to a change in popular consciousness. It would

---

134. D. RUDHYAR, DIRECTIVES FOR NEW LIFE 21-23 (1971).
135. *See* Stone, note 111 *supra*.

be a modest move, to be sure, but one in furtherance of a large goal: the future of the planet as we know it.

How far we are from such a state of affairs, where the law treats "environmental objects" as holders of legal rights, I cannot say. But there is certainly intriguing language in one of Justice Black's last dissents, regarding the Texas Highway Department's plan to run a six-lane expressway through a San Antonio Park.[136] Complaining of the Court's refusal to stay the plan, Black observed that "after today's decision, the people of San Antonio and the birds and animals that make their home in the park will share their quiet retreat with an ugly, smelly stream of traffic. . . . Trees, shrubs, and flowers will be mown down."[137] Elsewhere he speaks of the "burial of public parks," of segments of a highway which "devour parkland," and of the park's heartland.[138] Was he, at the end of his great career, on the verge of saying—just saying—that "nature has 'rights' on its own account"? Would it be so hard to do?

---

136. San Antonio Conservation Soc'y v. Texas Highway Dep't, *cert. denied*, 400 U.S. 968 (1970) (Black, J. dissenting to denial of certiorari).

137. *Id.* at 969.

138. *Id.* at 971.

# PART II

*Opinions of the U.S. Supreme Court*

# SUPREME COURT OF THE UNITED STATES

Syllabus

## SIERRA CLUB *v.* MORTON, SECRETARY OF THE INTERIOR, ET AL.

CERTIORARI TO THE UNITED STATES COURT OF APPEALS FOR
THE NINTH CIRCUIT

No. 70–34.   Argued November 17, 1971—Decided April 19, 1972

Petitioner, a membership corporation with "a special interest in the
conservation and sound maintenance of the national parks, game
refuges, and forests of the country," brought this suit for a declaratory judgment and an injunction restraining federal officials from
approving an extensive skiing development in the Mineral King
Valley in the Sequoia National Forest. Petitioner relies on § 10
of the Administrative Procedure Act, which accords judicial review to a "person suffering legal wrong because of agency action,
or [who is] adversely affected or aggrieved by agency action
within the meaning of a relevant statute." On the theory that
this was a "public" action involving questions as to the use of
natural resources, petitioner did not allege that the challenged
development would affect the club or its members in their activities or that they used Mineral King, but maintained that the
project would adversely change the area's aesthetics and ecology.
The District Court granted a preliminary injunction. The Court
of Appeals reversed, holding that the club lacked standing, and
had not shown irreparable injury. *Held:* A person has standing
to seek judicial review under the Administrative Procedure Act
only if he can show that he himself has suffered or will suffer
injury, whether economic or otherwise. In this case, where petitioner asserted no individualized harm to itself or its members,
it lacked standing to maintain the action. Pp. 4–14.

433 F. 2d 24, affirmed.

STEWART, J., delivered the opinion of the Court, in which
BURGER, C. J., and WHITE and MARSHALL, JJ., joined. DOUGLAS,
BRENNAN, and BLACKMUN, JJ., filed dissenting opinions. POWELL
and REHNQUIST, JJ., took no part in the consideration or decision
of the case.

57

# SUPREME COURT OF THE UNITED STATES

## No. 70–34

| | |
|---|---|
| Sierra Club, Petitioner,<br>*v.*<br>Rogers C. B. Morton, Individually, and as Secretary of the Interior of the United States, et al. | On Writ of Certiorari to the United States Court of Appeals to the Ninth Circuit. |

[April 19, 1972]

MR. JUSTICE STEWART delivered the opinion of the Court.

### I

The Mineral King Valley is an area of great natural beauty nestled in the Sierra Nevada Mountains in Tulare County, California, adjacent to Sequoia National Park. It has been part of the Sequoia National Forest since 1926, and is designated as a National Game Refuge by special Act of Congress.[1] Though once the site of extensive mining activity, Mineral King is now used almost exclusively for recreational purposes. Its relative inaccessibility and lack of development have limited the number of visitors each year, and at the same time have preserved the valley's quality as a quasi-wilderness area largely uncluttered by the products of civilization.

The United States Forest Service, which is entrusted with the maintenance and administration of national forests, began in the late 1940's to give consideration to Mineral King as a potential site for recreational de-

---

[1] Act of July 3, 1926, 44 Stat. 821, 16 U. S. C. § 688.

velopment. Prodded by a rapidly increasing demand for skiing facilities, the Forest Service published a prospectus in 1965, inviting bids from private developers for the construction and operation of a ski resort that would also serve as a summer recreation area. The proposal of Walt Disney Enterprises, Inc., was chosen from those of six bidders, and Disney received a three-year permit to conduct surveys and explorations in the valley in connection with its preparation of a complete master plan for the resort.

The final Disney plan, approved by the Forest Service in January, 1969, outlines a $35 million complex of motels, restaurants, swimming pools, parking lots, and other structures designed to accommodate 14,000 visitors daily. This complex is to be constructed on 80 acres of the valley floor under a 30-year use permit from the Forest Service. Other facilities, including ski lifts, ski trails, a cog-assisted railway, and utility installations, are to be constructed on the mountain slopes and in other parts of the valley under a revocable special use permit. To provide access to the resort, the State of California proposes to construct a highway 20 miles in length. A section of this road would traverse Sequoia National Park, as would a proposed high-voltage power line needed to provide electricity for the resort. Both the highway and the power line require the approval of the Department of the Interior, which is entrusted with the preservation and maintenance of the national parks.

Representatives of the Sierra Club, who favor maintaining Mineral King largely in its present state, followed the progress of recreational planning for the valley with close attention and increasing dismay. They unsuccessfully sought a public hearing on the proposed development in 1965, and in subsequent correspondence with officials of the Forest Service and the Department of the Interior, they expressed the Club's objections to Disney's plan as a whole and to particular features included in it.   In June of 1969 the Club filed the present suit in the United States District Court for the Northern District of California, seeking a declaratory judgment that various aspects of the proposed development contravene federal laws and regulations governing the preservation of national parks, forests, and game refuges,[2] and also seeking preliminary and permanent injunctions restraining the federal officials involved from granting their approval or issuing permits in connection with the Mineral King project.   The petitioner Sierra Club sued as a membership corporation with "a special interest in the conservation and sound maintenance of the national parks, game refuges, and forests of the country," and invoked the judicial review provisions of the Administrative Procedure Act, 5 U. S. C. § 701 *et seq.*

After two days of hearings, the District Court granted the requested preliminary injunction. It rejected the respondents' challenge to the Sierra Club's standing to sue, and determined that the hearing had raised questions "concerning possible excess of statutory authority,

---

[2] As analyzed by the District Court, the complaint alleged violations of law falling into four categories.  First, it claimed that the special use permit for construction of the resort exceeded the maximum acreage limitation placed upon such permits by 16 U. S. C. § 497, and that issuance of a "revocable" use permit was beyond the authority of the Forest Service.  Second, it challenged the proposed permit for the highway through Sequoia National Park on the grounds that the highway would not serve any of the purposes of the park in alleged violation of 16 U. S. C. § 1, and that it would destroy timber and other natural resources protected by 16 U. S. C. §§ 41 and 43.  Third, it claimed that the Forest Service and the Department of the Interior had violated their own regulations by failing to hold adequate public hearings on the proposed project. Finally, the complaint asserted that 16 U. S. C. § 45 (c) requires specific congressional authorization of a permit for construction of a power transmission line within the limits of a national park.

sufficiently substantial and serious to justify a preliminary injunction . . . ." The respondents appealed, and
the Court of Appeals for the Ninth Circuit reversed.
433 F. 2d 24. With respect to the petitioner's standing, the court noted that there was "no allegation in
the complaint that members of the Sierra Club would
be affected by the actions of [the respondents] other
than the fact that the actions are personally displeasing or distasteful to them," *id.,* at 33, and concluded:

> "We do not believe such club concern without a
> showing of more direct interest can constitute
> standing in the legal sense sufficient to challenge
> the exercise of responsibilities on behalf of all the
> citizens by two cabinet level officials of the gov-
> ernment acting under Congressional and Consti-
> tutional authority." *Id.,* at 30.

Alternatively, the Court of Appeals held that the Sierra
Club had not made an adequate showing of irreparable
injury and likelihood of success on the merits to justify issuance of a preliminary injunction. The court
thus vacated the injunction. The Sierra Club filed a
petition for a writ of certiorari which we granted, 401
U. S. 907, to review the questions of federal law
presented.

## II

The first question presented is whether the Sierra
Club has alleged facts that entitle it to obtain judicial
review of the challenged action. Whether a party has
a sufficient stake in an otherwise justiciable controversy
to obtain judicial resolution of that controversy is what
has traditionally been referred to as the question of
standing to sue. Where the party does not rely on any
specific statute authorizing invocation of the judicial
process, the question of standing depends upon whether
the party has alleged such a "personal stake in the out-

come of the controversy," *Baker* v. *Carr,* 369 U. S. 186, 204, as to ensure that "the dispute sought to be adjudicated will be presented in an adversary context and in a form historically viewed as capable of judicial resolution." *Flast* v. *Cohen,* 392 U. S. 83, 101. Where, however, Congress has authorized public officials to perform certain functions according to law, and has provided by statute for judicial review of those actions under certain circumstances, the inquiry as to standing must begin with a determination of whether the statute in question authorizes review at the behest of the plaintiff.[3]

The Sierra Club relies upon § 10 of the Administrative Procedure Act (APA), 80 Stat. 392, 5 U. S. C. § 702, which provides:

> "A person suffering legal wrong because of agency action, or adversely affected or aggrieved by agency action within the meaning of a relevant statute, is entitled to judicial review thereof."

Early decisions under this statute interpreted the language as adopting the various formulations of "legal

---

[3] Congress may not confer jurisdiction on Art. III federal courts to render advisory opinions, *Muskrat* v. *United States,* 219 U. S. 346, or to entertain "friendly" suits, *United States* v. *Johnson,* 319 U. S. 302, or to resolve "political questions," *Luther* v. *Borden,* 7 How. 1, because suits of this character are inconsistent with the judicial function under Art. III. But where a dispute is otherwise justiciable, the question whether the litigant is a "proper party to request an adjudication of a particular issue," *Flast* v. *Cohen,* 392 U. S. 83, 100, is one within the power of Congress to determine. Cf. *FCC* v. *Sanders Bros. Radio Station,* 309 U. S. 470, 477; *Flast* v. *Cohen,* 392 U. S. 83, 120 (Harlan, J., dissenting); *Associated Industries* v. *Ickes,* 134 F. 2d 694, 704. See generally Berger, Standing to Sue in Public Actions: Is it a Constitutional Requirement?, 78 Yale L. J. 816, 837 ff. (1969); Jaffe, The Citizen as Litigant in Public Actions: The Non-Hohfeldian or Ideological Plaintiff, 116 U. Pa. L. Rev. 1033 (1968).

interest" and "legal wrong" then prevailing as constitutional requirements of standing.[4]  But, in *Association of Data Processing Service Organizations, Inc.* v. *Camp*, 397 U. S. 150, and *Barlow* v. *Collins*, 397 U. S. 157, decided the same day, we held more broadly that persons had standing to obtain judicial review of federal agency action under § 10 of the APA where they had alleged that the challenged action had caused them "injury in fact," and where the alleged injury was to an interest "arguably within the zone of interests to be protected or regulated" by the statutes that the agencies were claimed to have violated.[5]

In *Data Processing,* the injury claimed by the petitioners consisted of harm to their competitive position in the computer servicing market through a ruling by the Comptroller of the Currency that national banks might perform data processing services for their customers.  In *Barlow,* the petitioners were tenant farmers who claimed that certain regulations of the Secretary of Agriculture adversely affected their economic position *vis-à-vis* their landlords.  These palpable economic injuries have long been recognized as sufficient to lay the basis for standing, with or without a specific statutory provision for judicial review.[6]  Thus, neither *Data Processing* nor *Barlow* addressed itself to the question, which has arisen with increasing frequency in federal courts

---

[4] See, *e. g., Kansas City Power & Light Co.* v. *McKay*, 225 F. 2d 924, 932; *Ove Gustavsson Contracting Co.* v. *Floete*, 278 F. 2d 912, 914; *Duba* v. *Schuetzle*, 303 F. 2d 570, 574.  The theory of a "legal interest" is expressed in its extreme form in *Alabama Power Co.* v. *Ickes*, 302 U. S. 464, 479–481.  See also *Tennessee Electric Power Co.* v. *TVA*, 306 U. S. 118, 137–139.

[5] In deciding this case we do not reach any questions concerning the meaning of the "zone of interests" test or its possible application to the facts here presented.

[6] See, *e. g., Hardin* v. *Kentucky Utilities Co.*, 390 U. S. 1, 7; *Chicago* v. *Atchison, T. & S. F. R. Co.*, 357 U. S. 77, 83; *FCC* v. *Sanders Bros. Radio Station,* 309 U. S. 470, 477.

in recent years, as to what must be alleged by persons
who claim injury of a noneconomic nature to interests
that are widely shared.[7] That question is presented
in this case.

## III

The injury alleged by the Sierra Club will be in-
curred entirely by reason of the change in the uses to
which Mineral King will be put, and the attendant
change in the aesthetics and ecology of the area. Thus,
in referring to the road to be built through Sequoia
National Park, the complaint alleged that the development "would destroy or otherwise affect the scenery,
natural and historic objects and wildlife of the park
and would impair the enjoyment of the park for future
generations." We do not question that this type of
harm may amount to an "injury in fact" sufficient to
lay the basis for standing under § 10 of the APA.
Aesthetic and environmental well-being, like economic
well-being, are important ingredients of the quality of
life in our society, and the fact that particular environmental interests are shared by the many rather than
the few does not make them less deserving of legal
protection through the judicial process. But the "injury
in fact" test requires more than an injury to a cognizable
interest. It requires that the party seeking review be
himself among the injured.

The impact of the proposed changes in the environment of Mineral King will not fall indiscriminately
upon every citizen. The alleged injury will be felt
directly only by those who use Mineral King and Sequoia

[7] No question of standing was raised in *Citizens to Preserve Overton Park, Inc.* v. *Volpe,* 401 U. S. 402. The complaint in that case
alleged that the organizational plaintiff represented members who
were "residents of Memphis, Tennessee who use Overton Park as a
park land and recreation area and who have been active since 1964
in efforts to preserve and protect Overton Park as a park land and
recreation area."

National Park, and for whom the aesthetic and recreational values of the area will be lessened by the highway and ski resort. The Sierra Club failed to allege that it or its members would be affected in any of their activities or pastimes by the Disney development. Nowhere in the pleadings or affidavits did the Club state that its members use Mineral King for any purpose, much less that they use it in any way that would be significantly affected by the proposed actions of the respondents.[8]

---

[8] The only reference in the pleadings to the Sierra Club's interest in the dispute is contained in paragraph 3 of the complaint, which reads in its entirety as follows:

"Plaintiff Sierra Club is a non-profit corporation organized and operating under the laws of the State of California, with its principal place of business in San Francisco, California since 1892. Membership of the Club is approximately 78,000 nationally, with approximately 27,000 members residing in the San Francisco Bay area. For many years the Sierra Club by its activities and conduct has exhibited a special interest in the conservation and sound maintenance of the national parks, game refuges and forests of the country, regularly serving as a responsible representative of persons similarly interested. One of the principal purposes of the Sierra Club is to protect and conserve the national resources of the Sierra Nevada Mountains. Its interests would be vitally affected by the acts hereinafter described and would be aggrieved by those acts of the defendants as hereinafter more fully appears."

In an *amici curiae* brief filed in this Court by the Wilderness Society and others, it is asserted that the Sierra Club has conducted regular camping trips into the Mineral King area, and that various members of the Club have used and continue to use the area for recreational purposes. These allegations were not contained in the pleadings, nor were they brought to the attention of the Court of Appeals. Moreover, the Sierra Club in its reply brief specifically declines to rely on its individualized interest, as a basis for standing. See n. 15, *infra*. Our decision does not, of course, bar the Sierra Club from seeking in the District Court to amend its complaint by a motion under Rule 15, Federal Rules of Civil Procedure.

The Club apparently regarded any allegations of individualized injury as superfluous, on the theory that this was a "public" action involving questions as to the use of natural resources, and that the Club's longstanding concern with and expertise in such matters were sufficient to give it standing as a "representative of the public." [9]  This theory reflects a misunderstanding of our cases involving so-called "public actions" in the area of administrative law.

The origin of the theory advanced by the Sierra Club may be traced to a dictum in *Scripps-Howard Radio, Inc.* v. *FCC,* 316 U. S. 4, in which the licensee of a radio station in Cincinnati, Ohio, sought a stay of an order of the FCC allowing another radio station in a nearby city to change its frequency and increase its range.  In discussing its power to grant a stay, the Court noted that "these private litigants have standing only as representatives of the public interest." *Id.,* at 14.  But that observation did not describe the basis upon which the appellant was allowed to obtain judicial review as a "person aggrieved" within the meaning of the statute involved in that case,[10] since Scripps-Howard was clearly "aggrieved" by reason of the economic injury that it would suffer as a result of the

---

[9] This approach to the question of standing was adopted by the Court of Appeals for the Second Circuit in *Citizens Committee for the Hudson Valley* v. *Volpe,* 425 F. 2d 97, 105:

"We hold, therefore, that the public interest in environmental resources—an interest created by statutes affecting the issuance of this permit—is a legally protected interest affording these plaintiffs, as responsible representatives of the public, standing to obtain judicial review of agency action alleged to be in contravention of that public interest."

[10] The statute involved was § 402 (b) (2) of the Communications Act of 1934, 48 Stat. 1064, 1093.

Commission's action.[11]  The Court's statement was rather directed to the theory upon which Congress had authorized judicial review of the Commission's actions. That theory had been described earlier in *FCC* v. *Sanders Bros. Radio Station*, 309 U. S. 470, 477, as follows:

> "Congress had some purpose in enacting § 402 (b)(2). It may have been of opinion that one likely to be financially injured by the issue of a license would be the only person having a sufficient interest to bring to the attention of the appellate court errors of law in the action of the Commission in granting the license. It is within the power of Congress to confer such standing to prosecute an appeal."

Taken together, *Sanders* and *Scripps-Howard* thus established a dual proposition: the fact of economic injury is what gives a person standing to seek judicial review under the statute, but once review is properly invoked, that person may argue the public interest in support of his claim that the agency has failed to comply with its statutory mandate.[12]  It was in the latter sense that the "standing" of the appellant in *Scripps-Howard* existed only as a "representative of the public interest."  It is in a similar sense that we have used the phrase "private attorney general" to describe the function performed by persons upon whom Congress has conferred the right to seek judicial re-

---

[11] This much is clear from the *Scripps-Howard* Court's citation of *FCC* v. *Sanders Bros. Radio Station*, 309 U. S. 470, in which the basis for standing was the competitive injury that the appellee would have suffered by the licensing of another radio station in its listening area.

[12] The distinction between standing to initiate a review proceeding, and standing to assert the rights of the public or of third persons once the proceeding is properly initiated, is discussed in 3 Davis, Administrative Law Treatise, §§ 22.05–22.07 (1958).

view of agency action. See *Data Processing, supra,*
at 154.

The trend of cases arising under the APA and other
statutes authorizing judicial review of federal agency
action has been towards recognizing that injuries other
than economic harm are sufficient to bring a person
within the meaning of the statutory language, and towards discarding the notion that an injury that is
widely shared is *ipso facto* not an injury sufficient to
provide the basis for judicial review.[13]  We noted this
development with approval in *Data Processing, supra,*
at 154, in saying that the interest alleged to have been
injured "may reflect 'aesthetic, conservational, and recreational' as well as economic values."  But broaden-
ing the categories of injury that may be alleged in support of standing is a different matter from abandoning
the requirement that the party seeking review must
have himself suffered an injury.

Some courts have indicated a willingness to take
this latter step by conferring standing upon organizations that have demonstrated "an organizational interest
in the problem" of environmental or consumer protection.  *Environmental Defense Fund, Inc. v. Hardin,* 428

---

[13] See, *e. g., Environmental Defense Fund, Inc. v. Hardin,* 428
F. 2d 1093, 1097 (interest in health affected by decision of Secretary
of Agriculture refusing to suspend registration of certain pesticides
containing DDT); *Office of Communication of the United Church
of Christ v. FCC,* 359 F. 2d 994, 1005 (interest of television viewers
in the programming of a local station licensed by the FCC); *Scenic
Hudson Preservation Conf. v. FPC,* 354 F. 2d 608, 615–616 (interests in aesthetics, recreation, and orderly community planning
affected by FPC licensing of a hydroelectric project); *Reade* v.
*Ewing,* 205 F. 2d 630, 631–632 (interest of consumers of oleo-
margarine in fair labeling of product regulated by Federal Security
Administration); *Crowther* v. *Seaborg,* 312 .F. Supp. 1205, 1212
(interest in health and safety of persons residing near the site of
a proposed atomic blast).

F. 2d 1093, 1097.[14]   It is clear that an organization whose members are injured may represent those members in a proceeding for judicial review.   See, *e. g.*, *NAACP* v. *Button*, 371 U. S. 415, 428.   But a mere "interest in a problem," no matter how longstanding the interest and no matter how qualified the organization is in evaluating the problem, is not sufficient by itself to render the organization "adversely affected" or "aggrieved" within the meaning of the APA.   The Sierra Club is a large and long-established organization, with an historic commitment to the cause of protecting our Nation's natural heritage from man's depredations.   But if a "special interest" in this subject were enough to entitle the Sierra Club to commence this litigation, there would appear to be no objective basis upon which to disallow a suit by any other bona fide "special interest" organization, however small or short-lived.   And if any group with a bona fide "special interest" could initiate such litigation, it is difficult to perceive why any individual citizen with the same bona fide special interest would not also be entitled to do so.

The requirement that a party seeking review must allege facts showing that he is himself adversely af-

---

[14] See *Citizens Committee for the Hudson Valley* v. *Volpe*, n. 8, *supra; Environmental Defense Fund, Inc.* v. *Corps of Engineers*, 325 F. Supp. 728, 734–736; *Izaac Walton League* v. *St. Clair*, 313 F. Supp. 1312, 1317.   See also *Scenic Hudson Preservation Conf.* v. *FPC, supra,* at 616:

"In order to ensure that the Federal Power Commission will adequately protect the public interest in the aesthetic, conservational, and recreational aspects of power development, those who by their activities and conduct have exhibited a special interest in such areas, must be held to be included in the class of 'aggrieved' parties under § 313 (b) [of the Federal Power Act]."

In most, if not all of these cases, at least one party to the proceeding did assert an individualized injury either to himself or, in the case of an organization, to its members.

fected does not insulate executive action from judicial review, nor does it prevent any public interests from being protected through the judicial process.[15]  It does serve as at least a rough attempt to put the decision as to whether review will be sought in the hands of those who have a direct stake in the outcome. That goal would be undermined were we to construe the APA to authorize judicial review at the behest of organizations or individuals who seek to do no more than vindicate their own value preferences through the judicial process.[16]  The principle that the Sierra Club would have us establish in this case would do just that.

---

[15] In its reply brief, after noting the fact that it might have chosen to assert individualized injury to itself or to its members as a basis for standing, the Sierra Club states:

"The Government seeks to create a 'heads I win, tails you lose' situation in which either the courthouse door is barred for lack of assertion of a private, unique injury or a preliminary injunction is denied on the ground that the litigant has advanced private injury which does not warrant an injunction adverse to a competing public interest.  Counsel have shaped their case to avoid this trap."

The short answer to this contention is that the "trap" does not exist.  The test of injury in fact goes only to the question of standing to obtain judicial review.  Once this standing is established, the party may assert the interests of the general public in support of his claims for equitable relief.  See n. 12 and accompanying text, *supra.*

[16] Every schoolboy may be familiar with de Tocqueville's famous observation, written in the 1830's, that "Scarcely any political question arises in the United States that is not resolved, sooner or later, into a judicial question."  1 Democracy in America 280 (Alfred A. Knopf, 1945).  Less familiar, however, is de Tocqueville's further observation that judicial review is effective largely because it is not available simply at the behest of a partisan faction, but is exercised only to remedy a particular, concrete injury.

"It will be seen, also, that by leaving it to private interest to censure the law, and by intimately uniting the trial of the law with the trial of an individual, legislation is protected from wanton

As we conclude that the Court of Appeals was correct in its holding that the Sierra Club lacked standing to maintain this action, we do not reach any other questions presented in the petition, and we intimate no view on the merits of the complaint.  The judgment is

*Affirmed.*

Mr. Justice Powell and Mr. Justice Rehnquist took no part in the consideration or decision of this case.

---

assaults and from the daily aggressions of party spirit.  The errors of the legislator are exposed only to meet a real want; and it is always a positive and appreciable fact that must serve as the basis for a prosecution." *Id.,* at 102.

# SUPREME COURT OF THE UNITED STATES

## No. 70–34

Sierra Club, Petitioner,

*v.*

Rogers C. B. Morton, Individually, and as Secretary of the Interior of the United States, et al.

On Writ of Certiorari to the United States Court of Appeals to the Ninth Circuit.

[April 19, 1972]

Mr. Justice Douglas, dissenting.

I share the views of my Brother Blackmun and would reverse the judgment below.

The critical question of "standing" [1] would be simplified and also put neatly in focus if we fashioned a federal rule that allowed environmental issues to be litigated before federal agencies or federal courts in the name of the inanimate object about to be dispoiled, defaced, or invaded by roads and bulldozers and where injury is the subject of public outrage. Contemporary public concern for protecting nature's ecological equilibrium should lead to the conferral of standing upon environmental objects to sue for their own preservation. See Stone, Should Trees Have Standing? Toward Legal Rights for Natural Objects, 45 S. Cal. L. Rev. 450 (1972). This suit would therefore be more properly labeled as *Mineral King* v. *Morton*.

Inanimate objects are sometimes parties in litigation. A ship has a legal personality, a fiction found useful for

---

[1] See generally *Data Processing Service* v. *Camp*, 397 U. S. 150 (1970); *Barlow* v. *Collins*, 397 U. S. 159 (1970); *Flast* v. *Cohen*, 392 U. S. 83 (1968). See also Mr. Justice Brennan's concurring opinion in *Barlow* v. *Collins, supra*, at 167. The issue of statutory standing aside, no doubt exists that "injury in fact" to "aesthetic" and "conservational" interests is here sufficiently threatened to satisfy the case or controversy clause. *Data Processing Service* v. *Camp, supra*, at 154.

73

maritime purposes.[2]   The corporation sole—a creature of
ecclesiastical law—is an acceptable adversary and large
fortunes ride on its cases.[3]   The ordinary corporation is
a "person" for purposes of the adjudicatory processes,
whether it represents proprietary, spiritual, aesthetic, or
charitable causes.[4]

So it should be as respects valleys, alpine meadows,
rivers, lakes, estuaries, beaches, ridges, groves of trees,

---

[2] *In rem* actions brought to adjudicate libellants' interests in
vessels are well known in admiralty.   Gilmore & Black, The Law
of Admiralty 31 (1957).   But admiralty also permits a salvage action
to be brought in the name of the rescuing vessel.   *The Comanche*,
75 U. S. (8 Wall.) 449, 476 (1869).   And, in collision litigation, the
first-libelled ship may counterclaim in its own name.   *The Gylfe* v.
*The Trujillo*, 209 F. 2d 386 (CA2 1954).   Our case law has personi-
fied vessels:

"A ship is born when she is launched, and lives so long as her identity
is preserved.   Prior to her launching she is a mere congeries of wood
and iron. . . .   In the baptism of launching she receives her name,
and from the moment her keel touches the water she is transformed. . . .   She acquires a personality of her own." *Tucker* v.
*Alexandroff*, 183 U. S. 424, 438

[3] At common law, an office holder, such as a priest or the King,
and his successors constituted a corporation sole, a legal entity
distinct from the personality which managed it.   Rights and duties
were deemed to adhere to this device rather than to the office
holder in order to provide continuity after the latter retired.   The
notion is occasionally revived by American courts.   E. g., *Reid* v.
*Barry*, 93 Fla. 849, 112 So. 846 (1927), discussed in Note, 12 Minn.
L. Rev. 295 (1928), and in Note, 26 Mich. L. Rev. 545 (1928);
see generally 1 Fletcher Cyclopedia Corporation, §§ 50–53; P. Potter,
Law of Corporation 27 (1881).

[4] Early jurists considered the conventional corporation to be a
highly artificial entity.   Lord Coke opined that a corporation's
creation "rests only in intendment and consideration of the law."
The Case of Suttons Hospital, 77 Eng. Rep. 937, 973 (K. B. 1613).
Mr. Chief Justice Marshall added that the device is "an artificial
being, invisible, intangible, and existing only in contemplation of
law." *Trustees of Dartmouth College* v. *Woodward*, 17 U. S.
(4 Wheat.) 518, 636 (1819).   Today suits in the names of corporations are taken for granted.

swampland, or even air that feels the destructive pressures of modern technology and modern life. The river, for example, is the living symbol of all the life it sustains or nourishes—fish, aquatic insects, water ouzels, otter, fisher, deer, elk, bear, and all other animals, including man, who are dependent on it or who enjoy it for its sight, its sound, or its life. The river as plaintiff speaks for the ecological unit of life that is part of it. Those people who have a meaningful relation to that body of water—whether it be a fisherman, a canoeist, a zoologist, or a logger—must be able to speak for the values which the river represents and which are threatened with destruction.

I do not know Mineral King. I have never seen it nor travelled it, though I have seen articles describing its proposed "development" [5] notably Hano, *Protectionists* v. *Recreationists*—the Battle of Mineral King,

---

[5] Although in the past Mineral King Valley has annually supplied about 70,000 visitor-days of simpler and more rustic forms of recreation—hiking, camping and skiing (without lifts)—the Forest Service in 1949 and again in 1965 invited developers to submit proposals to "improve" the Valley for resort use. Walt Disney Productions won the competition and transformed the Service's idea into a mammoth project 10 times its originally proposed dimensions. For example, while the Forest Service prospectus called for an investment of at least $3 million and a sleeping capacity of at least 100, Disney will spend $35.3 million and will bed down 3300 persons by 1978. Disney also plans a nine-level parking structure with two supplemental lots for automobiles, 10 restaurants and 20 ski lifts. The Service's annual license revenue is hitched to Disney's profits. Under Disneys' projections, the Valley will be forced to accommodate a tourist population twice as dense as that in Yosemite Valley on a busy day. And, although Disney has bought up much of the private land near the project, another commercial firm plans to transform an adjoining 160-acre parcel into a "piggyback" resort complex, further adding to the volume of human activity the Valley must endure. See generally; Note, Mineral King Valley: Who Shall Watch the Watchman?, 25 Rutgers L. Rev. 103, 107 (1970); Thar's Gold in Those Hills, 206 The Nation 260 (1968). For a general critique of mass recreation enclaves in national forests see Christian Science Monitor,

N. Y. Times Mag., Aug. 17, 1969; and Browning, Mickey Mouse in the Mountains, Harper's, March 1972, p. 65. The Sierra Club in its complaint alleges that "One of the principal purposes of the Sierra Club is to protect and conserve the national resources of the Sierra Nevada Mountains." The District Court held that this uncontested allegation made the Sierra Club "sufficiently aggrieved" to have "standing" to sue on behalf of Mineral King.

Mineral King is doubtless like other wonders of the Sierra Nevada such as Tuolumne Meadows and the John Muir Trail. Those who hike it, fish it, hunt it, camp in it, or frequent it, or visit it merely to sit in solitude and wonderment are legitimate spokesmen for it, whether they may be a few or many. Those who have that intimate relation with the inanimate object about to be injured, polluted, or otherwise despoiled are its legitimate spokesmen.

The Solicitor General, whose views on this subject are in the Appendix to this opinion, takes a wholly different approach. He considers the problem in terms of "government by the Judiciary." With all respect, the problem is to make certain that the inanimate objects, which are the very core of America's beauty, have spokesmen before they are destroyed. It is, of course, true that most of them are under the control of a federal or state agency. The standards given those agencies are usually expressed in terms of the "public interest." Yet "public interest" has so many differing shades of meaning as to be quite

---

Nov. 22, 1965, at 5, col. 1. Michael Frome cautions that the national forests are "fragile" and "deteriorate rapidly with excessive recreation use" because "(t)he trampling effect alone eliminates vegatative growth, creating erosion and water runoff problems. The concentration of people, particularly in horse parties, on excessively steep slopes that follow old Indian or cattle routes, has torn up the landscape of the High Sierras in California and sent tons of wilderness soil washing downstream each year." M. Frome, The Forest Service 69 (1971).

meaningless on the environmental front. Congress accordingly has adopted ecological standards in the National Environmental Policy Act of 1969, Pub. L. 91–90, 83 Stat. 852, 42 U. S. C. § 4321, *et seq.*, and guidelines for agency action have been provided by the Council on Environmental Quality of which Russell E. Train is Chairman. See 36 Fed. Reg. 7724.

Yet the pressures on agencies for favorable action one way or the other are enormous. The suggestion that Congress can stop action which is undesirable is true in theory; yet even Congress is too remote to give meaningful direction and its machinery is too ponderous to use very often. The federal agencies of which I speak are not venal or corrupt. But they are notoriously under the control of powerful interests who manipulate them through advisory committees, or friendly working relations, or who have that natural affinity with the agency which in time develops between the regulator and the regulated.[6] As early as 1894, Attorney General Olney

---

[6] The federal budget annually includes about $75 million for underwriting about 1,500 advisory committees attached to various regulatory agencies. These groups are almost exclusively composed of industry representatives appointed by the President or by Cabinet members. Although public members may be on these committees, they are rarely asked to serve. Senator Lee Metcalf warns: "Industry advisory committees exist inside most important federal agencies, and even have offices in some. Legally, their function is purely as kibitzer, but in practice many have become internal lobbies—printing industry handouts in the Government Printing Office with taxpayers' money, and even influencing policies. Industry committees perform the dual function of stopping government from finding out about corporations while at the same time helping corporations get inside information about what government is doing. Sometimes, the same company that sits on an advisory council that obstructs or turns down a government questionnaire is precisely the company which is withholding information the government needs in order to enforce a law." Metcalf, The Vested Oracles: How Industry Regulates Government, 3 The Washington Monthly 45 (1971). For proceedings conducted by Senator Metcalf exposing these relationships,

predicted that regulatory agencies might become "industry-minded," as illustrated by his forecast concerning the Interstate Commerce Commission:

> "The Commission is or can be made of great use to the railroads. It satisfies the public clamor for supervision of the railroads, at the same time that supervision is almost entirely nominal. Moreover, the older the Commission gets to be, the more likely it is to take a business and railroad view of things." M. Josephson, The Politicos 526 (1938).

Years later a court of appeals observed, "the recurring question which has plagued public regulation of industry [is] whether the regulatory agency is unduly oriented toward the interests of the industry it is designed to regulate, rather than the public interest it is supposed to protect." *Moss* v. *CAB*, 430 F. 2d 891, 893 (CADC 1970). See also *Office of Communication of the United Church of Christ* v. *FCC*, 359 F. 2d 994,

---

see Hearings on S. 3067 before the Subcommittee on Intergovernmental Relations of the Senate Committee on Government Operations, 91st Cong., 2d Sess. (1970); Hearings on S. 1737, S. 1964, and S. 2064 before the Subcommittee on Intergovernmental Relations of the Senate Committee on Government Operations, 92d Cong., 1st Sess. (1971).

The web spun about administrative agencies by industry representatives does not depend, of course, solely upon advisory committees for effectiveness. See Elman, Administrative Reform of the Federal Trade Commission, 59 Geo. L. J. 777, 788 (1971); Johnson, A New Fidelity to the Regulatory Ideal, 59 Geo. L. J. 869, 874, 906 (1971); R. Berkman & K. Viscusi, Damming The West, The Ralph Nadar Study Group Report On The Bureau of Reclamation 155 (1971); R. Fellmeth, The Interstate Commerce Omission, Ralph Nader Study Group on the Interstate Commerce Commission and Transportation 15–39 and *passim* (1970); J. Turner, The Chemical Feast, The Ralph Nader Study Group on Food Protection and the Food and Drug Administration *passism* (1970); Massel, The Regulatory Process, 26 Law and Contemporary Problems 181, 189 (1961); J. Landis, Report on Regulatory Agencies to the President-Elect 13, 69 (1960).

1003–1004; *Udall* v. *FPC*, 387 U. S. 428; *Calvert Cliffs' Coordinating Committee, Inc.* v. *AEC*, 449 F. 2d 1109; *Environmental Defense Fund, Inc.* v. *Ruckelshaus*, 439 F. 2d 584; *Environmental Defense Fund, Inc.* v. *HEW*, 428 F. 2d 1083; *Scenic Hudson Preservation Conf.* v. *FPC*, 354 F. 2d 608, 620. But see Jaffe, The Federal Regulatory Agencies In a Perspective: Administrative Limitation In A Political Setting, 11 Bos. C. I. & C. Rev. 565 (1970) (labels "industry-mindedness" as "devil" theory).

The Forest Service—one of the federal agencies behind the scheme to despoil Mineral King—has been notorious for its alignment with lumber companies, although its mandate from Congress directs it to consider the various aspects of multiple use in its supervision of the national forests.[7]

---

[7] The Forest Reserve Act of 1897, 30 Stat. 34, 16 U. S. C. § 551, imposed upon the Secretary of the Interior the duty to "preserve the [national] forests . . . from destruction" by regulating their "occupancy and use." In 1905 these duties and powers were transferred to the Forest Service created within the Department of Agriculture by the Act of Feb. 1, 1905, 33 Stat. 628, 16 U. S. C. § 472. The phrase "occupancy and use" has been the cornerstone for the concept of "multiple use" of national forests, that is, the policy that uses other than logging were also to be taken into consideration in managing our 154 national forests. This policy was made more explicit by the 1960 Multiple Use and Sustained Yield Act, 74 Stat. 215, 43 U. S. C. § 315, which provides that competing considerations should include outdoor recreation, range, timber, watershed, wildlife and fish purposes. The Forest Service, influenced by powerful logging interests, has, however, paid only lip service to its multiple use mandate and has auctioned away millions of timberland acres without considering environmental or conservational interests. The importance of national forests to the construction and logging industries results from the type of lumber grown therein which is well suited to builders' needs. For example, Western acreage produces douglas fir (structural support) and ponderosa pine (plywood lamination). In order to preserve the total acreage and so-called "maturity" of timber, the annual size of a Forest Service harvest is supposedly equated with expected yearly reforestation. Nonethe-

The voice of the inanimate object, therefore, should not be stilled. That does not mean that the judiciary takes over the managerial functions from the federal

less, yearly cuts have increased from 5.6 billion board feet in 1950 to 13.74 billion in 1971. Forestry professionals challenge the Service's explanation that this 240% harvest increase is not really overcutting but instead has resulted from its improved management of timberlands. "Improved management" answer the critics is only a euphemism for exaggerated regrowth forecasts by the Service. N. Y. Times, Nov. 15, 1971, at 48, col. 1. Recent rises in lumber prices have caused a new round of industry pressure to auction more federally owned timber. See Wagner, Resources Report/Lumbermen, conservationists head for new battle over government timber, 3 Nat. J. 657 (1971).

Aside from the issue of how much timber should be cut annually, another crucial question is *how* lumber should be harvested. Despite much criticism the Forest Service had adhered to a policy of permitting logging companies to "clearcut" tracts of auctioned acreage. "Clearcutting," somewhat analogous to strip mining, is the indiscriminate and complete shaving from the earth of all trees—regardless of size or age—often across hundreds of contiguous acres.

Of clearcutting Senator Gale McGee, a leading antagonist of Forest Service policy, complains: "The Forest Service's management policies are wreaking havoc with the environment. Soil is eroding, reforestation is neglected, if not ignored, streams are silting, and clearcutting remains a basic practice." N. Y. Times, Nov. 14, 1971, at 60, col. 2. He adds "In Wyoming . . . the Forest Service is very much nursemaid . . . to the lumber industry . . . ." Hearings on Management Practice on the Public Lands before the Subcommittee on Public Lands of the Senate Committee on Interior and Insular Affairs, pt. 1, at 7 (1971).

Senator Jennings Randolph offers a similar criticism of the leveling by lumber companies of large portions of the Monongahela National Forest in West Virginia. *Id.*, 9. See also 116 Cong. Rec. 36971 (1970) (reprinted speech of Sen. Jennings Randolph concerning Forest Service policy in Monongahela National Forest). To investigate similar controversy surrounding the Service's management of the Bitterroot National Forest in Montana, Senator Lee Metcalf recently asked forestry professionals at the University of Montana to study local harvesting practices. The faculty group concluded that public dissatisfaction had arisen from the Forest Service's "over-

agency. It merely means that before these priceless bits of Americana (such as a valley, an alpine meadow, a river, or a lake) are forever lost or are so transformed as to be reduced to the eventual rubble of our urban environment, the voice of the existing beneficiaries of these environmental wonders should be heard.[8]

---

riding concern for sawtimber production" and its "insensitivity to the related forest uses . . . and the public interest in environmental values." S. Doc. 91–115, 91st Cong., 2d Sess., 14 (1970). See also Behan, Timber Mining: Accusation or Prospect? 77 American Forests 4 (1971) (additional comments of faculty participant); Reich, The Public and the Nation's Forests, 50 Cal. L. Rev. 381–400 (1962).

Former Secretary of the Interior Walter Hickel similarly faulted clearcutting as excusable only as a money-saving harvesting practice for large lumber corporations. W. Hickel, Who Owns America? 130 (1971). See also Risser, the U. S. Forest Service; Smokey's Strip Miners, 3 The Washington Monthly 16 (1971). And at least one Forest Service study team shares some of these criticisms of clearcutting. U. S. Dept. of Agriculture, Forest Management in Wyoming 12 (1971). See also Public Land Law Review Comm'n, Report to the President and to the Congress 44 (1970); Chapman, Effects of Logging upon Fish Resources of the West Coast, 60 J. of For. 533 (1962).

A third category of criticism results from the Service's huge backlog of delayed reforestation projects. It is true that Congress has underfunded replanting programs of the Service but it is also true that the Service and lumber companies have regularly ensured that Congress fully fund budgets requested for the Forest Service's "timber sales and management." Frome, The Environment and Timber Resources, What's Ahead for Our Public Lands? 24 (A. Pyles ed. 1970).

[8] Permitting a court to appoint a representative of an inanimate object would not be significantly different from customary judicial appointments of guardians *ad litem*, executors, conservators, receivers, or counsel for indigents.

The values that ride on decisions such as the present one are often not appreciated even by the so-called experts.

"A teaspoon of living earth contains 5 million bacteria, 20 million fungi, one million protozoa, and 200,000 algae. No living human

Perhaps they will not win. Perhaps the bulldozers of "progress" will plow under all the aesthetic wonders of this beautiful land. That is not the present question. The sole question is, who has standing to be heard?

---

can predict what vital miracles may be locked in this dab of life, this stupendous reservoir of genetic materials that have evolved continuously since the dawn of the earth. For example, molds have existed on earth for about 2 billion years. But only in this century did we unlock the secret of the penicillins, tetracyclines, and other antibiotics from the lowly molds, and thus fashion the most powerful and effective medicines ever discovered by man. Medical scientists still wince at the thought that we might have inadvertently wiped out the rhesus monkey, medically, the most important research animal on earth. And who knows what revelations might lie in the cells of the blackback gorilla nesting in his eyrie this moment in the Virunga Mountains of Rwanda? And what might we have learned from the European lion, the first species formally noted (in 80 A. D.) as extinct by the Romans?

"When a species is gone, it is gone forever. Nature's genetic chain, billions of years in the making, is broken for all time." 13 Conserv. 4 (Nov. 1971).

Aldo Leopold wrote in Round River (1953) p. 147:

"In Germany there is a mountain called the Spessart. Its south slope bears the most magnificent oaks in the world. American cabinetmakers, when they want the last word in quality, use Spessart oak. The north slope, which should be better, bears an indifferent stand of Scotch pine. Why? Both slopes are part of the same state forest; both have been managed with equally scrupulous care for two centuries. Why the difference?

"Kick up the litter under the oaks and you will see that the leaves rot almost as fast as they fall. Under the pines, though, the needles pile up as a thick duff; decay is much slower. Why? Because in the Middle Ages the south slope was preserved as a deer forest by a hunting bishop; the north slope was pastured, plowed, and cut by settlers, just as we do with our woodlots in Wisconsin and Iowa today. Only after this period of abuse something happened to the microscopic flora and fauna of the soil. The number of species was greatly reduced, i. e., the digestive apparatus of the soil lost some of its parts. Two centuries of conservation have not sufficed to restore

Those who hike the Appalachian Trail into Sunfish Pond, New Jersey, and camp or sleep there, or run the Allagash in Maine, or climb the Guadalupes in West Texas, or who canoe and portage the Quetico Superior in Minnesota, certainly should have standing to defend those natural wonders before courts or agencies, though they live 3,000 miles away. Those who merely are caught up in environmental news or propaganda and flock to defend these waters or areas may be treated differently. That is why these environmental issues should be tendered by the inanimate object itself. Then there will be assurances that all of the forms of life [9] which it represents will stand before the court—the pileated woodpecker as well as the coyote and bear, the lemmings as well as the trout in the streams. Those inarticulate members of the ecological group cannot speak. But those people who have so frequented the place as to know its values and wonders will be able to speak for the entire ecological community.

Ecology reflects the land ethic; and Aldo Leopold wrote in A Sand County Almanac 204 (1949), "The

---

these losses. It required the modern microscope, and a century of research in soil science, to discover the existence of these 'small cogs and wheels' which determine harmony or disharmony between men and land in the Spessart."

[9] Senator Cranston has introduced a bill to establish a 35,000 acre Pupfish National Monument to honor the pupfish which are one inch long and are useless to man. S. 2141, 92d Cong., 1st Sess. They are too small to eat and unfit for a home aquarium. But as Michael Frome has said:

"Still, I agree with Senator Cranston that saving the pupfish would symbolize our appreciation of diversity in God's tired old biosphere, the qualities which hold it together and the interaction of life forms. When fishermen rise up united to save the pupfish they can save the world as well." Field & Stream, December 1971, p. 74.

land ethic simply enlarges the boundaries of the community to include soils, waters, plants, and animals, or collectively, the land."

That, as I see it, is the issue of "standing" in the present case and controversy.

# APPENDIX TO OPINION OF DOUGLAS, J.

Statement of the Solicitor-General:

.          .          .          .

"As far as I know, no case has yet been decided which holds that a plaintiff which merely asserts that, to quote from the complaint here, its interest would be widely affected, and that 'it would be aggrieved,' by the acts of the defendant, has standing to raise legal questions in court.

"But why not? Do not the courts exist to decide legal questions? And are they not the most impartial and learned agencies we have in our governmental system? Are there not many questions which must be decided by courts? Why should not the courts decide any question which any citizen wants to raise? As the tenor of my argument indicates, this raises, I think, a true question, perhaps a somewhat novel question, in the separation of powers. . . .

"Ours is not a government by the Judiciary. It is a government of three branches, each of which was intended to have broad and effective powers subject to checks and balances. In litigable cases, the courts have great authority. But the Founders also intended that the Congress should have wide powers, and that the executive branch should have wide powers. All these officers have great responsibilities. They are no less sworn than are the members of this Court to uphold the Constitution of the United States.

"This, I submit, is what really lies behind the standing doctrine, embodied in those cryptic words 'case' and 'controversy' in Article III of the Constitution. Analytically, one could have a system of government in which every legal question arising in the course of government would be decided by the courts. It would not be, I submit, a good system. More important, it is not the system which was ordained and established in our Constitution, as it has been understood for nearly 200 years.

"Over the past 20 or 25 years there has been a great shift in the decision of legal questions in our governmental operations into the courts. This has been the result of continuous whittling away of the numerous doctrines which have been established over the years, designed to minimize the number of governmental questions which it was the responsibility of the courts to consider.

"I have already mentioned the most ancient of all, case or controversy, which was early relied on to prevent the presentation of feigned issues to the court. But there are many other doctrines, which I cannot go into in detail: reviewability, justiciability, sovereign immunity, mootness in various aspects, statutes of limitations and laches, jursdictional amount, real party in interest and various questions in relation to joinder. Under all of these headings, limitations which previously existed to minimize the number of questions decided in courts have broken down in varying degrees. I might also mention the explosive development of class actions which has thrown more and more issues into the courts. . . .

"If there is standing in this case, I find it very difficult to think of any legal issue arising in government which will not have to await one or more decisions of the court before the administrator sworn to uphold the law, can take any action. I'm not sure that this is good for the government. I'm not sure that it is good for the courts. I do find myself more and more sure that it is not the kind of allocation of governmental power in our tripartite constitutional system that was contemplated by the Founders. . . .

"I do not suggest that administrators can act at their whim and without any check at all. On the contrary, in this area they are subject to continuous check by the Congress. Congress can stop this development any time it wants to."

# SUPREME COURT OF THE UNITED STATES

No. 70–34

Sierra Club, Petitioner,

*v.*

Rogers C. B. Morton, Individually, and as Secretary of the Interior of the United States, et al.

On Writ of Certiorari to the United States Court of Appeals to the Ninth Circuit.

[April 19, 1972]

MR. JUSTICE BRENNAN, dissenting.

I agree that the Sierra Club has standing for the reasons stated by my Brother BLACKMUN in Alternative No. 2 of his dissent. I therefore would reach the merits. Since the Court does not do so, however, I simply note agreement with my Brother BLACKMUN that the merits are substantial.

# SUPREME COURT OF THE UNITED STATES

---

No. 70–34

---

Sierra Club, Petitioner,
v.
Rogers C. B. Morton, Individually, and as Secretary of the Interior of the United States, et al.

On Writ of Certiorari to the United States Court of Appeals to the Ninth Circuit.

[April 19, 1972]

MR. JUSTICE BLACKMUN, dissenting.

The Court's opinion is a practical one espousing and adhering to traditional notions of standing as somewhat modernized by *Association of Data Processing Service Organizations, Inc.* v. *Camp,* 397 U. S. 150 (1970); *Barlow* v. *Collins,* 397 U. S. 159 (1970); and *Flast* v. *Cohen,* 392 U. S. 83 (1968). If this were an ordinary case, I would join the opinion and the Court's judgment and be quite content.

But this is not ordinary, run-of-the-mill litigation. The case poses—if only we choose to acknowledge and reach them—significant aspects of a wide, growing and disturbing problem, that is, the Nation's and the world's deteriorating environment with its resulting ecological disturbances. Must our law be so rigid and our procedural concepts so inflexible that we render ourselves helpless when the existing methods and the traditional concepts do not quite fit and do not prove to be entirely adequate for new issues?

The ultimate result of the Court's decision today, I fear, and sadly so, is that the 35.3-million-dollar complex, over 10 times greater than the Forest Service's suggested minimum, will now hastily proceed to completion; that serious opposition to it will recede in discouragement; and that Mineral King, the "area of great natural beauty

89

nestled in the Sierra Nevada Mountains," to use the
Court's words, will become defaced, at least in part, and,
like so many other areas, will cease to be "uncluttered
by the products of civilization."

I believe this will come about because: (1) The District Court, although it accepted standing for the Sierra
Club and granted preliminary injunctive relief, was reversed by the Court of Appeals, and this Court now up-
holds that reversal.   (2) With the reversal, interim relief
by the District Court is now out of the question and a
permanent injunction becomes most unlikely.   (3) The
Sierra Club may not choose to amend its complaint or,
if it does desire to do so, may not, at this late date, be
granted permission.   (4) The ever-present pressure to
get the project underway will mount.   (5) Once underway, any prospect of bringing it to a halt will grow
dim.   Reasons, most of them economic, for not stopping
the project will have a tendency to multiply.   And the
irreparable harm will be largely inflicted in the earlier
stages of construction and development.

Rather than pursue the course the Court has chosen
to take by its affirmance of the judgment of the Court
of Appeals, I would adopt one of two alternatives:

1. I would reverse that judgment and, instead, approve
the judgment of the District Court which recognized
standing in the Sierra Club and granted preliminary relief.   I would be willing to do this on condition that the
Sierra Club forthwith amend its complaint to meet the
specifications the Court prescribes for standing.   If Sierra
Club fails or refuses to take that step, so be it; the case
will then collapse.   But if it does amend, the merits will
be before the trial court once again.   As the Court's
footnote 2, *ante,* p. 3,*so clearly reveals, the issues on
the merits are substantial and deserve resolution.   They
assay new ground.   They are crucial to the future of
Mineral King.   They raise important ramifications for

* (Editor's note: see p. 61 in this book.)

the quality of the country's public land management. They pose the propriety of the "dual permit" device as a means of avoiding the 80-acre "recreation and resort" limitation imposed by Congress in 16 U. S. C. § 497, an issue that apparently has never been litigated, and is clearly substantial in light of the congressional expansion of the limitation in 1956 arguably to put teeth into the old, unrealistic five-acre limitation. In fact, they concern the propriety of the 80-acre permit itself and the consistency of the entire, enormous development with the statutory purposes of the Sequoia Game Refuge, of which the Valley is a part. In the context of this particular development, substantial questions are raised about the use of National Park area for Disney purposes for a new high speed road and a 66,000-volt power line to serve the complex. Lack of compliance with existing administrative regulations is also charged. These issues are not shallow or perfunctory.

2. Alternatively, I would permit an imaginative expansion of our traditional concepts of standing in order to enable an organization such as the Sierra Club, possessed, as it is, of pertinent, bona fide and well-recognized attributes and purposes in the area of environment, to litigate environmental issues. This incursion upon tradition need not be very extensive. Certainly, it should be no cause for alarm. It is no more progressive than was the decision in *Data Processing* itself. It need only recognize the interest of one who has a provable, sincere, dedicated, and established status. We need not fear that Pandora's box will be opened or that there will be no limit to the number of those who desire to participate in environmental litigation. The courts will exercise appropriate restraints just as they have exercised them in the past. Who would have suspected 20 years ago that the concepts of standing enunciated in *Data Processing* and *Barlow* would be the measure for

today? And MR. JUSTICE DOUGLAS, in his eloquent
opinion, has imaginatively suggested another means and
one, in its own way, with obvious, appropriate and self-
imposed limitations as to standing. As I read what he
has written, he makes only one addition to the customary
criteria (the existence of a genuine dispute; the assur-
ance of adversariness; and a conviction that the party
whose standing is challenged will adequately represent
the interests he asserts), that is, that the litigant be one
who speaks knowingly for the environmental values he
asserts.

I make two passing references:

1. The first relates to the Disney figures presented to
us. The complex, the Court notes, will accommodate
14,000 visitors *a day* (3,100 overnight; some 800 employees; 10 restaurants; 20 ski lifts). The State of
California has proposed to build a new road from Ham-
mond to Mineral King. That road, to the extent of
9.2 miles, is to traverse Sierra National Park. It will
have only two lanes, with occasional passing areas, but
it will be capable, it is said, of accommodating 700–800
vehicles per hour and a peak of 1,200 per hour. We
are told that the State has agreed not to seek any further improvement in road access through the park.

If we assume that the 14,000 daily visitors come by
automobile (rather than by helicopter or bus or other
known or unknown means) and that each visiting automobile carries four passengers. (an assumption, I am
sure, that is far too optimistic), those 14,000 visitors will
move in 3,500 vehicles. If we confine their movement
(as I think we properly may for this mountain area) to
12 hours out of the daily 24, the 3,500 automobiles will
pass any given point on the two-lane road at the rate
of about 300 per hour. This amounts to five vehicles
per minute, or an average of one every 12 seconds. This
frequency is further increased to one every six seconds

when the necessary return traffic along that same two-lane road is considered. And this does not include service vehicles and employees' cars. Is this the way we perpetuate the wilderness and its beauty, solitude and quiet?

2. The second relates to the fairly obvious fact that any resident of the Mineral King area—the real "user"— is an unlikely adversary for this Disney-governmental project. He naturally will be inclined to regard the situation as one that should benefit him economically. His fishing or camping or guiding or handyman or general outdoor prowess perhaps will find an early and ready market among the visitors. But that glow of anticipation will be short-lived at best. If he is a true lover of the wilderness—as is likely, or he would not be near Mineral King in the first place—it will not be long before he yearns for the good old days when masses of people—that 14,000 influx per day—and their thus far uncontrollable waste were unknown to Mineral King.

Do we need any further indication and proof that all this means that the area will no longer be one "of great natural beauty" and one "uncluttered by the products of civilization?" Are we to be rendered helpless to consider and evaluate allegations and challenges of this kind because of procedural limitations rooted in traditional concepts of standing? I suspect that this may be the result of today's holding. As the Court points out, *ante,* pp. 11–12,* other federal tribunals have not felt themselves so confined.[1] I would join those progressive holdings.

---

[1] *Environmental Defense Fund, Inc.* v. *Hardin,* 428 F. 1093, 1096–1097 (CADC 1970); *Citizens for the Hudson Valley* v. *Volpe,* 425 F. 2d 97, 101–105 (CA2 1970), cert. denied, 400 U. S. 949; *Scenic Hudson Preservation Conference* v. *FPC,* 354 F. 2d 608, 615–617 (CA2 1965); *Izaak Walton League* v. *St. Clair,* 313 F. Supp. 1312, 1316–1317 (Minn. 1970); *Environmenal Defense Fund, Inc.* v. *Corps*

---

* (Editor's note: see pp. 69–70 in this book.)

The Court chooses to conclude its opinion with a footnote reference to De Tocqueville. In this environmental context I personally prefer the older and particularly pertinent observation and warning of John Donne.[2]

---

of Engineers, 324 F. Supp. 878, 879–880 (DC 1971); Environmental Defense Fund, Inc. v. Corps of Engineers, 325 F. Supp. 728, 734–736 (ED Ark. 1971); Sierra Club v. Hardin, 325 F. Supp. 99, 107–112 (Alas. 1971); Upper Pecos Association v. Stans, 328 F. Supp. 332, 333–334 (N. Mex. 1971); Cape May County Chapter, Inc., Izaak Walton League v. Macchia, 329 F. Supp. 504, 510–514 (N. J. 1971).

See National Automatic Laundry & Cleaning Council v. Schultz, 443 F. 2d 689, 693–694 (CADC 1971); West Virginia Highlands Conservancy v. Island Creek Coal Co., 441 F. 2d 232, 234–235 (CA4 1971); Environmental Defense Fund, Inc. v. HEW, 428 F. 2d 1083, 1085 n. 2 (CADC 1970); Honchok v. Hardin, 326 F. Supp. 988, 991 (Md. 1971).

[2] "No man is an Iland, intire of itselfe; every man is a peece of the Continent, a part of the maine; if a Clod bee washed away by the Sea, Europe is the lesse, as well as if a Promontorie were, as well as if a Mannor of thy friends or of thine owne were; any man's death diminishes me, because I am involved in Mankinde; And therefore never send to know for whom the bell tolls; it tolls for thee." Devotions XVII.

# INDEX

# ABOUT THE AUTHOR

Christopher D. Stone, Professor of Law at the University of Southern California, did his undergraduate work at Harvard, graduating *magna cum laude* in Philosophy in 1959. After receiving his law degree from Yale, he proceeded to the University of Chicago, where he was Fellow in Law and Economics in 1962–63. He practiced law with a large Wall Street firm until 1965, when he moved to California to join the faculty at U.S.C., teaching courses that range from Legal Philosophy to Corporation Law.

Past Chairman of the Association of American Law School Committee on Law and the Humanities, Professor Stone is also a member of the American Society for Political and Legal Philosophy and has served as Consultant to the President's Task Force on Communications Policy. At present he is doing research, supported by the National Science Foundation, analyzing various legal and other social strategies for controlling corporate behavior.

Professor Stone has written numerous articles and is co-author of LAW, LANGUAGE & ETHICS (Foundation Press 1972). His next book will be a major study of the problems involved in the social control of the modern business corporation.